CULTURES OF THE W...
Sudan

Published in 2017 by Cavendish Square Publishing, LLC
243 5th Avenue, Suite 136, New York, NY 10016
Copyright © 2017 by Cavendish Square Publishing, LLC

Third Edition

This publication represents the opinions and views of the author based on his or her personal experience, knowledge, and research. The information in this book serves as a general guide only. The author and publisher have used their best efforts in preparing this book and disclaim liability rising directly or indirectly from the use and application of this book.
CPSIA Compliance Information: Batch #CS17CSQ
All websites were available and accurate when this book was sent to press.

Library of Congress Cataloging-in-Publication Data

Names: Levy, Patricia, 1951- author. | Latif, Zawiah Abdul. author. | Young-Brown, Fiona, author.
Title: Sudan / Patricia Levy, Zawiah Abdul Latif, and Fiona Young Brown.
Other titles: Cultures of the world.
Description: New York : Cavendish Square Publishing, 2017. | Series: Cultures of the world | Includes bibliographical references and index.
Identifiers: LCCN 2016056232 (print) | LCCN 2016057527 (ebook) | ISBN 9781502626110 (library bound) | ISBN 9781502626028 (E-book)
Subjects: LCSH: Sudan--Juvenile literature.
Classification: LCC DT154.6 .L482 2017 (print) | LCC DT154.6 (ebook) | DDC 962.4--dc23
LC record available at https://lccn.loc.gov/2016056232

Editorial Director: David McNamara
Editor: Kristen Susienka
Copy Editor: Nathan Heidelberger
Associate Art Director: Amy Greenan
Designer: Alan Sliwinski
Production Coordinator: Karol Szymczuk
Photo Research: J8 Media

PICTURE CREDITS

Printed in the United States of America

CONTENTS

SUDAN TODAY

LOCATED AT THE CROSSROADS OF THE ARAB AND THE AFRICAN worlds, Sudan has been an important site of religious and cultural diversity since ancient times. Once the largest nation on the African continent, it has been home to a number of ancient civilizations since as long ago as 3300 BCE. These included the Kush, the Meroë, and the Nubians, all of whom flourished along the Nile, the river that is the lifeblood of Africa. Kingdoms that matched those of ancient Egypt thrived, and so did trade, architecture, and agriculture. Monuments to a golden age gone by still stand upon the desert sands.

For centuries, Sudan was the target of many conquest attempts, both successful and unsuccessful. In 1821, northern Sudan came under Egyptian rule. It later fell into British hands and became a Crown colony in 1899. Under Anglo-Egyptian rule, Sudan became divided in many respects. The North was largely Muslim and Arabic-speaking, while the South was a combination of both Christian and animist peoples, with the English language more widespread. This division would repeatedly rear its head decades later with civil war and the push for South Sudanese separation.

The relationship between Egypt and Britain was often strained, with Sudan caught in the middle of their power struggle. After World War II, a legislature was established and the Sudanese were encouraged to choose between an alliance with Egypt or independence. They chose the latter.

In 1956, the country gained its independence from colonialism, but it has since struggled to create a place for itself on the world economic stage. Cultural, political, and economic imbalances between the North and South soon became inevitable. The first ruling coalition government to be elected after independence quickly broke down and the military seized power. The result has been two lengthy and divisive civil wars, the most recent of which literally split the country into two nations. Much of the ongoing fighting and rebellion was in the southern part of Sudan, where people resisted the imposition of strict Islamic law. They also protested food shortages and lack of economic and humanitarian support during periods of severe drought.

A Sudanese family is gathered outside their home.

South Sudan became an independent nation in 2011, six years after being allowed to create its own government. In addition to war, Sudan has been devastated by poverty and humanitarian crises. Scars of war and famine still run deep through the country's soul, but hope for a positive future remains.

In the twenty-first century, postwar Sudan is attempting to redefine itself. Following the secession of South Sudan, the country is working to rebuild its economy and make the most of its natural resources. With the fertile plains of the Nile, a supply of rich mineral and oil deposits, and a climate that is ideal for renewable energy, Sudan has the potential to be self-reliant, perhaps even wealthy. Nevertheless, many problems remain, both economic and cultural, and these are working against potential progress. Strong tensions remain between different regions, and progress is proving hard to maintain. Despite the secession of the southern region to form an autonomous South Sudan, conflicts continue to ravage the eastern and southern parts of the country. Meanwhile, government corruption means that many public resources are lacking. Many areas, particularly rural, are still without the most basic facilities such as clean water, reliable electricity, and access to health care.

However, the Sudanese people retain the resilience that has kept them strong for centuries. They produce critically acclaimed works of art, literature, and music. Their hospitality and dedication to community and family remain unblemished by past struggles. It is important for Sudan's people to continue to come together and celebrate their strengths if the nation is to overcome a painful legacy of war and hunger.

GEOGRAPHY

More than half of Sudan's land area is desert.

1

SUDAN IS THE THIRD-LARGEST country in Africa, slightly less than one-fifth the size of the United States, with a land area of nearly 719,000 square miles (1.86 million square kilometers). Only Algeria and the Democratic Republic of the Congo are larger. Until the secession of South Sudan in 2011, it was the largest country on the continent. The Red Sea lies along its northeastern border. Sudan shares borders with seven other countries: Egypt, Libya, Chad, the Central African Republic, Ethiopia, Eritrea, and South Sudan.

Sudan has a population of almost thirty-seven million people, one-third of whom live in urban areas. More than 50 percent of the country's total land area is desert. The northern part of the country is largely sand or gravel, being part of the lower Sahara and Nubian Deserts. South-central Sudan is marked by clay plains and the Nuba Mountains, while in the West, the Marrah Mountains rise from the Darfur Plateau. The Nile River flows from south to north along the entire length of the eastern half of the country.

The name Sudan comes from "Bilad al-Sudan," meaning "land of the black people," the name given to the region by nomadic Arabs in the Middle Ages.

THE LIFEBLOOD OF SUDAN

Giving Sudan its very existence, the Nile is the most important feature of life in the country. For some of its length, the Nile is made up of several rivers, among them the White Nile and the Blue Nile, which flow through or near Sudan. However, its waters, which can give life to the land, can also be destructive. The Nile is the longest river in the world: its most remote headstream is in Burundi, in central Africa, and from that point until it enters the Mediterranean Sea, the river is 4,145 miles (6,670 kilometers) long. The White Nile enters Sudan just beyond the South Sudan border town of Renk and flows north to Khartoum. The Blue Nile is the more turbulent of the two rivers. It has its origins in Lake Tana, a crater lake in the highlands of Ethiopia. It enters Sudan through a gorge that is almost 1 mile (1.5 km) deep in places. This gorge was not fully mapped until the 1960s because it is so

Wooden boats, known as feluccas, are used to carry goods and people along the Nile River.

difficult to access. The river crosses the flat, hot plains of eastern Sudan to join the White Nile at Khartoum. The Nile never dries up because the Blue Nile carries far more water than the White Nile. It provides most of the Middle Nile's water through the long, hot summers and irrigates about 70 percent of the irrigated land in Sudan.

Beyond Khartoum, the Nile flows over six groups of rapids, called cataracts, five of which are in Sudan. The final group is at Aswan in Egypt. Two hundred miles (322 km) north of Khartoum, the Nile meets the Atbara River, a minor tributary. One cataract is located near the confluence of these two rivers. The Nile continues to flow north from here but, at one point, switches direction to flow south, before once again curving back to the northern direction. The fourth cataract, in the Manasir Desert, lies at the midpoint of this large S-shaped curve, which is often called the "Great Bend."

THE MIDDLE NILE

The Middle Nile is a distinct geographical region that extends from the meeting of the Blue Nile and the White Nile at Khartoum to the First Cataract at Aswan in Egypt. In this region, the river is demarcated geographically by several cataracts (series of rapids).

The lifeblood of the region is the river itself. It is used for irrigation—water is pumped or dammed into irrigation systems—and deposits fertile soil in the Nile floodplain, which is cultivated in the drier seasons. Irrigation along the banks of the river creates a narrow strip of vegetation quite different from that of the surrounding area. In some places, the strip is only 109 yards (100 m) wide. In others, it is nonexistent—the desert comes right to the edge of the river. As a result of desert sandstorms, there is a buildup of sand on some of the west bank of the river. This shifting sand continually encroaches on irrigated fields and settlements.

On either side of this fertile, cultivated strip is a vast area of savanna (semiarid grassland) where the inhabitants are nomadic herders who travel around the area to find grazing land for their animals. Because drought and the encroaching desert have reduced the area of grassland, the herders have experienced serious hardship, loss of animals, and starvation.

DAMMING THE NILE

The English first built a dam at Aswan in 1899; its height was raised in 1912 and in 1933. A second, higher dam was built in the 1960s, which affected the lives of some fifty thousand Sudanese.

The Roseires Dam was built for irrigation but also features a power-generation plant.

As the waters rose, twenty-seven villages and the town of Wadi Halfa were submerged. The people were compensated and relocated at Khasm el Girba, east of Khartoum. Lake Nasser, also known as Lake Nubia in Sudan, created by the dam, is one of the world's largest reservoirs. Under an international agreement, the country of Sudan is allowed to draw 640 billion cubic feet (18.1 billion cubic meters) of water from Lake Nasser, making major development projects possible.

South of Khartoum are the Sennar Dam, built after World War I, and a dam on the White Nile at Jabal Awliya, built in 1937. The Roseires irrigation project, located on the Blue Nile and served by the Roseires Dam, has brought more than 865,511 acres (350,260 hectares) of land under cultivation.

SUDAN'S DESERTS

More than 50 percent of Sudan's land area is desert. To the west is the Libyan Desert, which has supplied vast amounts of oil farther west in Libya. The Nubian Desert is a region in northeast Sudan. The bits of fertile land along the Nile are known locally as Batn el Hagar, or "the belly of stones."

Sudan is undergoing a period of rapid desertification because of global climate change and the harsh demands being made on the savanna. Plants are unable to survive drought, the harvesting of firewood, and grazing by animals.

THE MOUNTAINS OF SUDAN

There are several major mountainous areas in Sudan. The Red Sea Hills in the northeast are low-lying stony hills near the coast. The terrain here is like that of the rest of northern Sudan. The Marrah Mountains in the West are distinctive, rounded pillars of rock that stand out over the lower wooded slopes. The mountain valleys have rich, fertile soil, making the region agriculturally productive. Sudan's highest peak, Mount Marrah, is part of this mountain range. It has a height of 10,075 feet (3,071 m). In the southern part of the country are the Nuba Mountains.

HOT AND DRY

Sudan is one of Africa's hottest countries. It lies within the tropics, but because of its size, Sudan sees a great range of climate conditions. The northern half

The Taka Mountains are a distinctive feature of the Kassala landscape in eastern Sudan.

The aardwolf, found in parts of Sudan, lives mainly on termites.

of the country, the Nubian and Libyan Deserts, are dry all year. They experience occasional flash thunderstorms that last just a few minutes and that, in some areas, may occur only once in a generation. Temperatures range from 100 degrees Fahrenheit to 113°F (38 degrees Celsius to 45°C) between May and September but can fall to almost 32°F (0°C) between November and March. Wind blows continually from the north, often whipping up sandstorms known as *haboobs* (ha-BOOBS), which last for a short time, darkening the sky and bringing gale-force winds. They are rarely accompanied by rain.

The lower half of the country experiences a hot and wet season and a hot and dry season. The southwest experiences the highest rainfall. The rainy season starts in April and lasts until November; it provides as much as 60 inches (152 centimeters) of rain per year. As one travels north, the rainy season grows shorter. Khartoum, at the very edge of the desert, has the least rain—on average about 4 inches (10 cm) between July and August, and only an average of 6.4 inches (16 cm) throughout the whole year. Temperatures are highest just before the rainy season and lowest during December and January. In Khartoum, the average temperature is 89°F (32°C) in July and 74°F (23°C) in December.

The Red Sea area has a humid climate determined by its position on the coast. It has two rainy seasons, one in the winter and the other corresponding to the summer rainy season of the Middle Nile.

VARIED WILDLIFE

Sudan has an enormous variety of wildlife, the result of its varied habitats—from the desert to the mountains along the border of the South and the lush river valleys of the Nile, where crocodiles and hippopotamuses thrive.

Haboob *is an Arabic word that means "blasting" or "drifting." It is used to refer to a type of strong dust storm. Haboobs are a common occurrence in areas with arid climates, such as the Sahara Desert in Sudan. This type of dust storm was named in Sudan, but they also happen in parts of the Arabian Peninsula, Australia, and even Texas and Arizona in the United States.*

When a thunderstorm forms, winds rush from all directions into the storm. When the storm collapses, rain begins to fall. At the same time, the winds change direction and gust out of the storm. This sudden draft of air hits the ground, stirring up all the loose dust and dirt into a wall that is pushed along in front of the storm. Often, in the heat of the desert, the rain evaporates before it even reaches the ground, so all that is left is the haboob—a giant wall of dust. Sometimes, a haboob can be up to 10,000 feet (3 km) high and up to 62 miles (100 km) wide. Smaller haboobs may only last for as little as ten minutes and travel just a few miles. However, stronger ones can last for several hours, traveling 100 miles (161 km) or more.

Sudan has historically been home to a multitude of wildlife, including lions, zebras, antelopes, primates, and elephants. Poaching of the latter led to a flourishing trade. Much of this wildlife was concentrated in what is now South Sudan. Sadly, ongoing conflicts and a lack of government interest in conservation means that up-to-date information is difficult to find.

We do know that the wildlife in the Nuba Mountains has suffered greatly. As part of a scorched-earth policy in the war against the Nuba, most of the animals that might have been hunted for food have been destroyed.

Throughout Sudan, a number of animal breeds are now listed as critically endangered or endangered. These include the African wild ass, the chimpanzee, Grevy's zebra, the slender-horned gazelle, and some other antelope, as well as smaller mammals. Many other species, including the African elephant, lion, cheetah, and Barbary sheep, are considered vulnerable.

PLANT LIFE

The flora of the region varies as widely as does its animal life. Much of the rain forest and papyrus swamps are now in South Sudan, although small pockets of these can be found in the far south of the country. Here, huge buttressed trees block out the sunlight and smaller shade-loving plants survive beneath. However, in much of Sudan, the plant life is dependent on the river for its survival, with thin strips of vegetation forming along the riverbanks.

In the Middle Nile are large areas of savanna, sandy soil covered by tall grasses and low, drought-resistant trees. The seasonal rains bring a sudden burst of life to the plants here. Of all the land in Sudan, the savanna is under the most intense pressure from drought, the cutting of firewood, and overgrazing.

Farther north, little plant life grows except during occasional rain showers that allow dormant seeds to quickly germinate, flower, and produce new seeds, which then lie dormant, waiting for the next rain.

Palm trees are a common sight along the banks of the Nile.

An interesting plant that grows in the South and the Middle Nile is the baobab tree. Its huge trunk can grow to a diameter of 30 feet (9 m). It produces an edible fruit that is made into a cooling drink. The bark is harvested for rope making.

Another plant with a multiplicity of uses is the date palm, which can be seen all along the banks of the Nile and in the oases. Besides its edible fruit, its leaves, fibers, trunk, and sap are used to make baskets, mats, crates, furniture, sawdust, brooms, rope, roof beams, footbridges, and wine.

CITIES

The capital city of Sudan is Khartoum. Khartoum and its neighboring cities of Omdurman and Khartoum North and their suburbs form a bustling metropolis with a population of about 5.1 million. These cities form the industrial, commercial, and communications center of Sudan.

There are several theories about the origin of the name Khartoum, including that it is the Arabic for "elephant trunk" (a reference to the Nile), Arabic for "safflower" (once an important crop), or perhaps that it is derived from the Beja word for "meeting."

Most of Sudan's imports and exports travel through Port Sudan, located on the coast of the Red Sea.

The British laid out Khartoum's gardens and tree-lined avenues, and many of the old colonial buildings built by the British are still in use, although they are rather shabby now. Beside these, more modern multistory buildings have sprung up. Omdurman and other parts of Khartoum are more Arab in style, with flat-roofed single-story houses, narrow alleyways, beautiful mosques, and of course the souk, the city market. Five bridges and outboard motorboats carry passengers and their goods between Khartoum, Omdurman, and Khartoum North. In the years of drought and war, many refugees from southern Sudan, Darfur, and neighboring countries came to Khartoum to live in poorly built shantytowns around the city's edge.

After the Khartoum metropolitan area, the next largest city in Sudan is Nyala, in South Darfur. Historically, it was the capital of the Daju Empire. Later, when Sudan was under the British Crown, the city was the site of the British Administration Headquarters. The city and the area surrounding it

Sudan's capital, Khartoum, has both Western-style high-rise and more traditional Arab-style buildings.

are of great archaeological importance, and it is believed that many ancient treasures are still to be discovered. Since the outbreak of conflict in Darfur, many refugees have fled toward Nyala, and a large refugee camp formed at the edge of the city.

Another large city in Sudan is Port Sudan, on the east coast. It was built to accommodate the trade across the Red Sea and to other coastal countries. Today, Port Sudan is the main export center for cotton, peanuts, and oil. An international airport and an oil refinery are located in proximity to the city.

Wadi Halfa, near the Egyptian border, survives on the trade between Egypt and Sudan. A considerable black market exists for scarce goods in this region. Buildings are traditional one-story flat-roofed structures, often enclosing a central courtyard with trees to create some shade in the searing heat of the afternoons.

INTERNET LINKS

http://www.independent.co.uk/travel/africa/the-complete-guide-to-the-nile-420928.html
This article provides a detailed guide to traveling the length of the Nile, including its communities and history.

http://peakery.com/region/sudan-mountains
This website lists the mountains of Sudan, including their location and height.

http://www.sudanembassy.org/index.php/about-sudan-sp-942178989
The Sudanese Embassy gives an introduction to Sudan at this website.

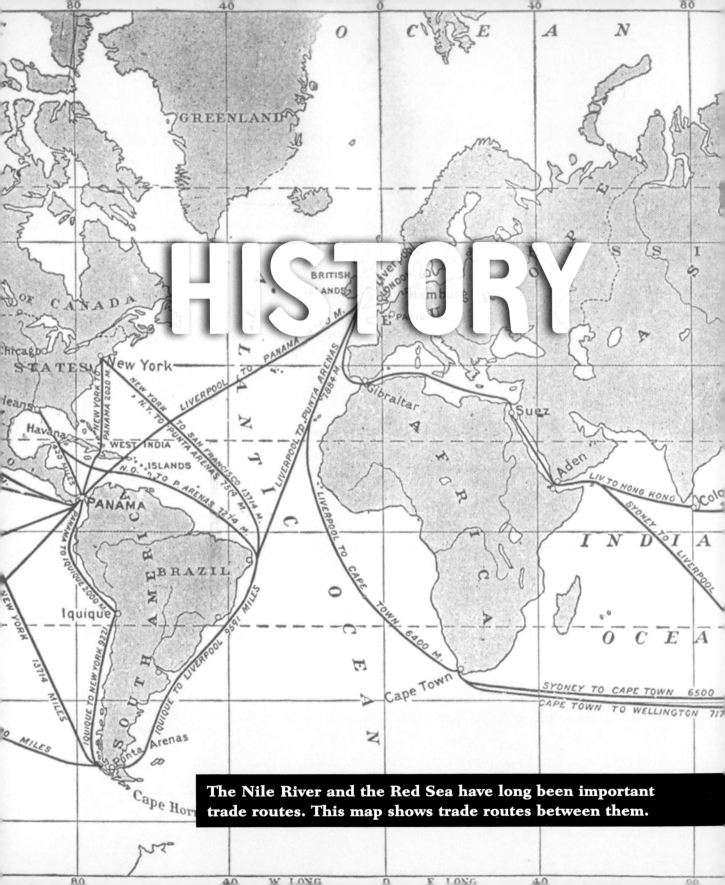

HISTORY

The Nile River and the Red Sea have long been important trade routes. This map shows trade routes between them.

S UDAN'S POSITION ON THE NILE AND
the Red Sea means it has played a
major role in the development of
international trading routes. Influences
from the East and the Mediterranean have
combined with those of Africa and Arabia
to produce a culturally diverse range of
traditions. In the North, the presence of
the Nubian Empire and its proximity to
Egypt have contributed to a rich, well-
recorded history. Although the history
of the southern and western areas is
less explored, archaeologists have found
evidence of many fascinating peoples.

DEVELOPING TRADE ROUTES

The area of modern Sudan known as the Middle Nile, from Khartoum
in the south to Aswan in the north, has had a special part to play in the
history of the world. The earliest cities in Africa south of Egypt, built by
the Kushite or Kerma civilization, developed along this stretch of the
Nile. North of the Middle Nile is the Middle East and Arab culture; south
lies the barrier of the Sudd, surrounded by "black" Africa. Historically,

the Nile was a major route into Africa, where ivory, gold, and slaves could be bought or taken. The area remained a major trade route until the development of camel routes across the Sahara in the first millennium CE, followed in the sixteenth century by sailing ships trading along the coasts of Africa.

EARLY CIVILIZATIONS

The earliest structures discovered in Sudan are in the region of the Third Cataract, separate from the modern Egyptian border. They are a series of palaces, temples, and residences built in the third millennium BCE by the ancient Nubians at Kerma.

The oldest city of the Kush civilization, Kerma was situated at the Third Cataract between about 2500 and 1500 BCE, a period when Egyptian influence was low. The small city was established in one of the rare areas where river water could be channeled easily to low-lying land. It is the earliest known non-Egyptian African city. It had a complex social structure and rulers who

Pyramids are not just found in Egypt; they were also important to the ancient civilizations of Sudan.

NUBIA

Nubia was one of the earliest-recorded African civilizations. Located in what is now northern Sudan and southern Egypt, the kingdom served as an important trading pathway from the southern parts of Africa to the Mediterranean and beyond. Nubia was first settled in approximately 5000 BCE. People were drawn by the fertile lands along the Nile. Soon, they had built a region rich in agricultural crops, cattle, and precious minerals, including gold. As the civilization grew, Nubian kings erected impressive cities, temples, and monuments. Archaeological excavations have also revealed a writing system, although it is not as well understood as other ancient languages. Nevertheless, records from Egypt and Greece mention complex relationships with the Nubian Empire.

were buried with large numbers of human sacrifices—the most ever found in burials anywhere in the world. The settlement included a huge cemetery, buildings used for storage and religious activities, a lightly fortified city, and craft centers. It is thought that the town was a transport and assembly point for exports from the southern Middle Nile into Egypt.

Around 1500 BCE, the Egyptian Empire's conquest in the Middle Nile extended almost as far as the Fifth Cataract. Fortified towns were gradually replaced by less-military settlements with temples dedicated to the Egyptian gods. This second wave of Egyptian influence in Kush ended around 1000 BCE, mainly because of political problems in Egypt itself, and possibly because of low water levels in the Nile, which would have made trade difficult.

KINGDOMS

Around the ninth century BCE, Kushite civilization was reborn with the Napata Kingdom, which has left behind the ruins of temples, cemeteries, and towns. At one time, around the eighth and seventh centuries BCE, this kingdom was so powerful it controlled the whole of Egypt. Napata's rulers were also called pharaohs and copied Egyptian customs; decorations in temple ruins show Egyptian gods with curly hair and African features. The society used Egyptian hieroglyphics, as is evident from tomb and temple inscriptions.

The Kingdom of Meroë came into existence around 400 BCE, as Napata declined, and lasted nearly seven hundred years. The ruins of Meroë reveal a palace with baths and plumbing, factories, houses, and evidence of an iron-smelting works. It was a civilization based on farming the banks of the Nile, which were lined with farms and small towns. Small pyramidal tombs held the bodies of kings and queens, and the Lion Temple has exterior paintings showing the rulers of Meroë with the Lion God.

Meroë existed concurrently with the Greek and Roman domination of Egypt. It was attacked by the Roman Empire in 23 BCE, suffered repeated attacks by nomadic groups in the following centuries, and was finally conquered by the Axumite Empire of Ethiopia in about 350 CE.

The Sudanese desert is still home to many ancient temples and elaborately carved columns.

THE SPREAD OF CHRISTIANITY

By about the sixth century CE, what is now northern Sudan was settled by three major kingdoms, all of which practiced Christianity. Christianity had spread through the Roman Empire into Egypt and, later, to Sudan and Ethiopia.

The Nubian Christian kingdoms built beautiful churches and extensive cities; the ruins of these cities are still being discovered. Elite houses in the cities had plumbing, indoor toilets, and frescoes on the walls, and the residents drank from imported glassware.

The human settlement of the Middle Nile region depended on the river. In one season the Nile could destroy crops and houses by flooding; the next it could be so low that the fields could not be irrigated and crops died. In one year it might bring rich soil up from the South to grow the next season's crops, while in another year it might wash all the arable soil away. There was also the problem of getting water to the arable land. Three types of land existed, each defined by the type of irrigation system it required.

Seluka land was situated on the floodplain of the river. Each year soil and water were carried up by the river, and all the farmer had to do was plant his crops, weed them, and watch them grow. The drawback of this land was that it could be cultivated only during one season.

Shadoof land was the next to develop. It was the land that lay 10 feet (3 m) or less above the river, so that water could be lifted up to it using a man-powered pivot.

Saquia land was around 25 feet (8 m) above the level of the river and came into cultivation only after the invention of the ox-drawn waterwheel.

A fourth type of land, rare in the Sudan, was basin land, which lay adjacent to the river but at a lower level. River water could be channeled into it by means of a canal or when the river overflowed.

THE BIRTH OF ISLAM

Gradually the Christian kingdoms gave way to a Muslim sultanate dominated by Arabs who brought their own religion—Islam. The largest of the sultanates was the Funj Kingdom of Sennar, which survived into the early nineteenth century. The Funj sultan's wealth came from slaves and gold mines close to the border with modern Ethiopia.

At the start of the nineteenth century, the Arab sheikhdoms of Sudan were attacked by the forces of the ruler of Egypt, Muhammad Ali. He had seized power in Egypt with the use of a Turkish slave army that he sent south with one of his sons to take slaves and gold. The troops ventured into and beyond the Sudd. They sent back thirty thousand slaves and the ears of those they killed. During the return journey, one of Ali's sons was killed, and

A poster from 1897 shows images from the British war in Sudan.

in retribution, Ali sent more troops and took control of Sudan. Egyptian rule lasted sixty-three years.

THE COLONIAL ERA

The construction of the Suez Canal in the nineteenth century attracted both British and French attention. The French were keen on assisting in the construction and established the Suez Canal Company in 1858. The construction of the canal used tens of thousands of people in forced labor. Meanwhile, the British viewed the French project as a threat to their geopolitical and financial interests. When Egypt not only went heavily into debt over the building of the Suez Canal but also failed to establish effective control over southern Sudan, it gave Britain the opportunity to intervene in the region. Forced labor was condemned, and the project was temporarily halted. In 1877, General Charles Gordon was appointed governor of Sudan and Egypt. He worked to bring an end to the region's slave trade, which affected not just the canal's construction but much of the area's economy. During his first year as governor, the Anglo-Egyptian Slave Trade Convention was signed, pledging to end the slave trade by 1880.

While the Turco-Egyptians and the British were establishing their authority, a local leader emerged. Muhammad Ahmad declared himself a Mahdi, or savior, elected by God to lead a jihad, or holy war. He called for Sudan to be ruled according to the laws of Islam. The Mahdi took the towns of Kordofan and Darfur by siege, killing the European and Turkish leaders, and starving out the troops. Hearing of the unrest, the British sent General Gordon to Khartoum to hold the city against the Mahdi. Gordon asked for reinforcements too late; the city was taken, and Gordon was killed. His head was put on a pole to taunt the relieving troops.

The Mahdists held power for thirteen years while Britain and other colonial powers conquered other regions of Africa, dividing up the land to be exploited. Eventually, a campaign against the Mahdists was organized. General Horatio Herbert Kitchener was sent with troops from Egypt, arriving in Omdurman on September 2, 1898. They were attacked by sixty thousand Mahdists armed with swords and shields and wearing suits of armor. Eleven thousand Sudanese died, and the British gained power in Sudan.

SUDANESE INDEPENDENCE

The Anglo-Egyptian Condominium remained in joint control of Sudan until World War II. In 1946, Britain and Egypt began negotiations to decide Sudan's future, but they ended in deadlock, as Egypt demanded British withdrawal, and Britain wanted to remain in control.

Muhammad Ahmad, also known as the Mahdi, was viewed by many Sudanese as a savior, leading them to freedom.

In 1948, the British began a process of giving Sudan the choice of union with Egypt or independence. They established a legislature, which the pro-Egyptians boycotted, and in December 1950 the legislature passed a motion asking Britain and Egypt for independence.

Meanwhile, the Egyptian National Assembly named King Farouk of Egypt the sole ruler of Sudan, but after his abdication in 1952, Egypt and Britain agreed to grant independence to Sudan. In 1953, the first elections were held, and a three-year period of replacing British and Egyptian officials with Sudanese began.

FIRST CIVIL WAR

At this stage, the enormous social and political differences between the North and the South began to make themselves felt even more acutely. During the British administration, the two halves of the country had been kept separate, but with the new pro-Egyptian party in power, southern elements began to see a threat to their control over their own affairs. In August 1955, a mutiny among southern regiments broke out.

The modern Sudanese flag

Sudan formally became a republic on January 1, 1956. Elections were held in February 1958, and the Umma Party, led by Abdallah Khalil, came to power. His government was formed from a coalition of small parties and was quite unstable. Within six months, interparty quarrels and national strikes ended the government.

Power was seized by General Ibrahim Abboud, the chief of staff of the armed forces. He outlawed strikes and political parties, and under his military government, which remained in power for six years, Sudan's economy began to improve.

A low-key rebellion continued in the South. Finally there was an unarmed mass rebellion against the military rulers, and they agreed to step down. Elections followed, and in May 1965, parliamentary rule was reestablished.

MILITARY COUP

In 1969 a second military coup brought Colonel Jaafar al-Nimeiry to power. Political parties were again banned, and a degree of economic stability returned. This military government withstood twenty-two attempted coups before the twenty-third one succeeded. One of the most optimistic aspects

of al-Nimeiry's rule was the peace accord he made with the southern forces at Addis Ababa in 1972, which gave the South a large amount of regional autonomy and halted the war.

Al-Nimeiry began a series of projects to make Sudan a major food supplier, including the Jonglei Canal project. But his loans from the International Monetary Fund caused dissent when he was forced to raise food prices to meet debt repayments.

To gain support wherever he could, al-Nimeiry turned to the conservative northern Islamic groups, declaring sharia law in 1983. This meant that every citizen throughout the country, regardless of religion, was bound by the laws of Islam.

Civil war has been an all-too-frequent part of modern Sudanese history.

SECOND CIVIL WAR

President Omar al-Bashir

Angered by the imposition of Islamic laws, the non-Muslim people in the South took up arms once more. They were led this time by John Garang, a US economics graduate, who formed the Sudan People's Liberation Army (SPLA). The northerners quickly lost control of the South. A state of emergency was declared, and the revolt expanded.

In 1985 there was a successful election, and Sayyid Sadiq al-Mahdi, great-grandson of the Mahdi, became the new leader of Sudan. For the next four years, there was a return to civilian parliamentary government and a purge of Islamic extremists. But sharia law continued, and food shortages and economic decline were made worse by the war and drought in the South. Another military coup took place in 1989, led by Brigadier Omar Hassan al-Bashir. He declared a state of emergency, political opposition was again suppressed, and the war against the South was stepped up. Moves toward democracy began again in 1993, and by 2002 al-Bashir had brokered a cease-fire with the SPLA with the Machakos Protocol, a statement of intent to end the war. Although there were disputes over sharing power, by 2003 hostilities were formally declared over, with al-Bashir remaining as president and Garang as vice president. Garang died shortly afterward in a plane crash. The peace deal was signed and finalized in Nairobi, giving regional autonomy to the South and ending more than twenty-two years of civil war. During this second war, as many as two million Sudanese died, mostly as a result of starvation and drought.

Since 2008, the International Criminal Court has made repeated calls for the arrest of President Omar al-Bashir on charges of genocide and war crimes. Sudan has ignored the charges. Al-Bashir continues to serve as president of Sudan, having been reelected in 2010 and 2015.

SOUTH SUDAN INDEPENDENCE

A key part of the peace accords ending the civil war gave greater political autonomy to South Sudan. In 2005, the region created its own government. At its head

An election worker displays a ballot at a local polling station.

was Salva Kiir Mayardit, head of the SPLA and successor to John Garang. Mayardit continued as president when South Sudan became an independent state in 2011. Secession from Sudan did not lead to immediate peace in the newly formed nation; as of 2016, South Sudan continues to navigate a fragile peace agreement.

UNREST IN DARFUR

Unfortunately, the peace process was overshadowed by armed rebellion in Darfur in the West. Having felt long ignored in the peace process, two new rebel groups, the Sudan Liberation Army (SLA) and the Justice and Equality Movement (JEM), attacked in 2003, seeking greater autonomy for the Fur, Masalit, and Zaghawa tribes. The government responded by arming Arab militias, the Janjaweed (JOHN-ja-weed), to put down the insurrection. More than two hundred thousand Arab and non-Arab people in the region were killed, and more than two million people fled from their homes. In May 2006 the SLA signed a peace agreement with the government, but the other rebel group rejected the offer. A further cease-fire agreement, signed in 2010 by

Rebel forces in the Darfur region

the Sudanese government and JEM, also failed. In June, 2011, a Darfur Peace Agreement was signed by all parties. However, little progress had been made by the following year, and violence escalated once again. During 2014, more than 3,300 villages were destroyed in 400,000 attacks by Sudanese soldiers and allies. As of 2016, the conflict continues, with reports of chemical weapons attacks against Darfur residents.

BORDER CONFLICT WITH CHAD

The Darfur conflict spilled over to neighboring Chad when Janjaweed militias and Chadian rebel groups, allegedly aided by the Sudanese government, raided villages in Abeché, in eastern Chad, in pursuit of two hundred thousand asylum-seeking Fur refugees. The raid displaced more than thirty thousand Chadian villagers and killed several others. In 2006, the Tripoli Agreement was signed to bring a cease-fire to the conflict, but rebel activities continued. A second agreement was signed in 2008. Two months later, diplomatic relations between the two nations were severed, although they were reinstated after six months. In 2010, the president of Chad visited Sudan, which led to a change in Chad's position on Darfur. Chad and Sudan agreed to share joint border patrols, on a rotating schedule.

After years of conflict, many Sudanese have been displaced from their homes and live in United Nations refugee camps.

INTERNET LINKS

http://www.darfurinfo.org
Visit this site to read news about the ongoing conflict in the Darfur region.

http://www.sudanembassy.org/index.php/history-of-the-sudan
This series of pages hosted by the Sudanese Embassy details the country's history through colonialism and independence to the present day.

https://oi.uchicago.edu/museum-exhibits/history-ancient-nubia
Hosted by the Oriental Institute at the University of Chicago, this web page details the history of Nubia and its early art.

GOVERNMENT

People stand before a courthouse in the capital city of Khartoum.

3

The National Anthem
of Sudan is called
"Nahnu Jund Allah
Jun Al-watan" ("We
are the soldiers
of God and of our
homeland").

SUDAN'S POLITICAL HISTORY IS widely varied. Before colonialism, Sudan was a series of small states ruled by individual kings. From 1898 to 1956, Anglo-Egyptian Sudan, as it was known, was under British rule.

Since gaining independence, the country has known both parliamentary democracy and military dictatorships. Different political groups have all been struggling to gain control for the last few decades. Some of these groups are marked by regional or ethnic diversity, others by religious or political ties. As a result, governments have often had to form coalitions with other groups. The Islamic influence of the North has been most strongly felt, and today Sudan follows sharia law. It was this imposition of sharia law in 1983 that led to civil war, and the eventual secession of South Sudan. The Comprehensive Peace Agreement (CPA) with the South was signed in January 2005, and in 2011 South Sudan became an independent nation. Today the government of Sudan is a presidential republic, with Omar Hassan al-Bashir having been in power as president since 1993.

A PRESIDENTIAL REPUBLIC

Sudan is officially a presidential republic, where all effective political power is in the hands of the president. In recent years it has been a one-party presidential republic, a military regime, a parliamentary democracy, another military regime, and a transitional state between military rule and parliamentary democracy.

**First Vice President
Bakri Hassan Saleh**

Currently, the National Congress Party (NCP) holds governmental power, having won 323 of the available parliamentary seats in the election of 2015. The NCP was formerly the National Islamic Front (NIF). In 1989, President Omar Hassan al-Bashir declared the NCP the only legally recognized political party. Multiparty politics would be reintroduced a decade later, but the NCP continues to dominate. Al-Bashir was reelected in 2015, winning 94.1 percent of the vote, although many Sudanese refused to vote, claiming the results were a foregone conclusion. Bakri Hassan Saleh is Sudan's first of two vice presidents, having been appointed in 2013. Saleh was part of the 1989 coup that gave al-Bashir power, and he is expected to succeed him to the presidency. The second vice president is Hassabu Mohamed Abdalrahman, also elected in 2013.

THE OFFICE OF PRESIDENT

The president theoretically holds office for five years, although in the past, coup attempts have often interrupted this process. After the 1985 coup, when Sudan spent a brief time as a democracy, there was no president. Instead, the role was carried out by a five-man Supreme Council.

Currently the presidency is held by General al-Bashir, who has led the country since 1989. He is also the commander in chief of the armed forces. He was "elected" in 1996 when a call was made for a new president and National Assembly. As president, al-Bashir has the power to suspend the constitution and declare a state of emergency, a prerogative that has been used several times by Sudanese presidents. In 1999, al-Bashir did call for a state of emergency and dissolved the National Assembly in the wake of parliament speaker al-Turabi's call for reducing the powers of the president and reestablishing the role of the prime minister. The National Assembly resumed in 2001 after al-Bashir was "reelected" in 2000 for a second term amid boycotts by the opposition and accusations of vote rigging. From 2005 to 2010, he oversaw a transitional coalition government between the NCP and the Sudan People's Liberation Movement (SPLM), as determined by peace accords. He was later reelected in 2010 (winning 68 percent of the vote) and in 2015. Both elections were surrounded by claims of corruption.

President al-Bashir meets the Egyptian president.

THE NATIONAL LEGISLATURE

Until 2011, the National Legislature was made up of the new version of the National Assembly, consisting of 450 president-appointed members, and the Council of States, consisting of 50 members indirectly elected by state legislatures. In 2015, the way in which National Legislature members were chosen changed, however. Now they are elected rather than appointed. The Council of States is made up of two representatives from each state. All members of the National Legislature serve a six-year term. However, after South Sudan's independence in 2011, the number of seats should have been reduced to 354. A total of 426 seats were available in the 2015 elections.

Currently, Sudan's National Legislature is dominated by al-Bashir's National Congress Party, which holds 76 percent of the seats. The Democratic Unionist Party holds a small number of seats. Opposition parties are allowed, but they have little chance of wielding any real power.

THE COURTS

The legal system in Sudan is generally based on sharia law. Some remnants of English common law remain, but Islamic law typically takes precedence.

SHARIA LAW

Sharia law is imposed throughout the country, although a few protections for non-Muslims were established in the 2005 peace accords. Sharia law seems to be inconsistent, varying according to the geography of the country.

Many penalties determined by sharia law apply to all citizens, regardless of their own religion. Public lashing is common for those found guilty of drinking alcohol or uttering blasphemy, for which the maximum sentence is one hundred lashes. For a theft of anything valued at more than forty dollars, the right hand is amputated. For aggravated theft or more serious crimes, the right hand and the left foot are amputated.

Adultery and repeated homosexuality are punishable by execution, but in both cases the enormous burden of proof has prevented these punishments from being carried out. Those convicted of "shameful" acts are lashed; this is quite common in cases of suspected adultery. Those found engaging in premarital sex are also lashed, with the guilty receiving the maximum one hundred lashes.

Those injured by crime can demand retribution. For example, a woman whose arm was broken can demand that the arm of the woman who caused the injury be broken also.

One notable case was that of a pregnant woman sentenced to death in 2014 for refusing to renounce her Christian faith. She was eventually freed after the case received international attention.

There are four levels of courts for civil issues and five for criminal issues. At the bottom of the hierarchy are the town benches, followed by the district court, the province courts, and the courts of appeal. At the top of the hierarchy is the Supreme Court, which is the final court of appeal. All National Supreme Court and Constitutional Court judges are appointed by the president, upon advice from the National Judicial Service Commission. A total of seventy judges serve on the National Supreme Court, while nine justices serve on the Constitutional Court.

SUDAN'S MILITARY

The Sudanese Armed Forces (SAF) make up Sudan's military arm. Historically, these forces received inadequate training and had limited and outdated equipment and poor maintenance capabilities. The situation was made worse in the 1990s with the dismissals of professional officer corps. At times, the government has had to enlist the assistance of rebel groups and Arab militias to fight insurrections. Today, Sudan's military defense is equipped with modern weapons from China and Russia. According to 2011 figures, it has 109,000 members. The army is the largest unit, followed by the air force and the navy. Together they are charged with the defense of Sudan's external borders and the preservation of internal security.

Sudanese soldiers wave the flag of their country in the city of Khartoum.

The Sudanese army is organized into ten divisions, including one armored, one mechanized, and six infantry divisions. The air force and the navy have an estimated 13,000 and 1,800 personnel respectively. The navy is based at Khartoum, Port Sudan, and Marsá Gwiyai.

STATE GOVERNMENT

The organization of local government has been through numerous changes. Between 1983 and 1997, the country was divided into eight regions, each headed by a military governor. In 1997, the eight regions were replaced with twenty-six states. Following South Sudan's independence in 2011, and the addition of two states within Darfur in 2012 and one in Kurdufan in 2013, there are currently eighteen states or administrative districts. Though state-level positions used to be filled by presidential appointment, local elections have been held since 2010.

HUMAN RIGHTS

Sudan has a record of human-rights abuses by both government and rebel forces. The government has placed restrictions on freedoms of assembly, speech, religious practice, and political association. The media and the judicial system are thus tightly controlled and subjected to government interference. Government security forces are also said to operate "ghost houses," secret detention centers where political opponents are taken for harsh interrogation. Amnesty International has recorded many cases of illegal detention and torture of political opponents of the government.

Amnesty International also blames both government and rebel forces for the "disappearance" of thousands of civilians in the South and the Nuba Mountains. More recently, in Darfur, the government and rebel forces have committed atrocities, murdering, raping, and driving millions of people from their homes into refugee camps. The delivery of humanitarian aid to the area is also restricted. In the North, the age-old practice of enslaving southern boys as young as twelve years old persists.

Many people in Darfur rely on international food aid.

POLITICAL PARTIES

Political parties in Sudan have undergone periods of being banned interspersed with periods of relative freedom. In 1998, the constitution permitted political "associations," provided that they were registered with the government.

The most prominent is the ruling party, the National Congress Party. Headed by President al-Bashir and Ibrahim Umar, it is the successor to the former National Islamic Front. The Democratic Unionist Party is a center-right party, dedicated to embracing a secular country in order to promote social pluralism. In the 2015 election, they won twenty-five seats. Several factions of the Umma Party also hold seats.

The Sudan People's Liberation Movement–North (SPLM–N) is currently banned in Sudan. It should not be confused with the SPLM, the political wing of the Sudan People's Liberation Army (SPLA) that sought independence for South Sudan. Although originally aligned, the two groups have since split. The SPLM–N comprises former SPLM members who remained in Sudan after 2011. Located in the states of Blue Nile and South Kordofan, they are actively engaged in armed insurgency against the current Sudanese regime.

INTERNET LINKS

https://www.amnesty.org/en/countries/africa/sudan/report-sudan
This link takes you to annually updated reports about human rights abuses, conflicts, and refugees.

http://www.nationsonline.org/oneworld/sudan-government.htm
Here you can find a list of Sudanese government agencies and ministries, with links to the appropriate web pages.

http://www.presidency.gov.sd
This is the official homepage of the Presidential Palace of Sudan.

ECONOMY

Cotton, an important crop in Sudan, is harvested by hand.

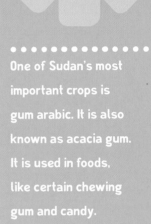

4

One of Sudan's most important crops is gum arabic. It is also known as acacia gum. It is used in foods, like certain chewing gum and candy.

SUDAN'S ECONOMY HAS RIDDEN many highs and lows since the 1960s, when there was zero economic growth. An unsteady government, two civil wars, and international sanctions have all taken their toll. In 1999, Sudan began exporting crude oil, a move that began to greatly improve the nation's economy. For the next decade, the economy boomed, thanks largely to oil production and resulting foreign investments in infrastructure. However, three-quarters of that production was based in South Sudan and therefore was lost in July 2011. Since then, Sudan has been struggling to compensate for that loss of revenue.

As of 2015, growth of the gross domestic product (GDP) had remained steady for several years at 3.5 percent, compared with 8.6 percent a decade earlier. The 2015 inflation rate was 17.3 percent, a significant improvement from the 2014 rate of 36.9 percent.

Conflict continues in Darfur and in the Blue Nile region. This has combined with famine, drought, corruption, and debt to worsen the

GUM ARABIC

One of Sudan's most important crops is gum arabic. Also known as acacia gum, it is a resin that comes from some varieties of the acacia tree, particularly those that grow in western Sudan. The resin seeps from the trees and hardens into walnut-sized balls. Harvesting begins in the middle of the rainy season and continues through the dry season. Gum arabic is used mainly in cooking, as a thickening agent and stabilizer. It is also used in the making of some adhesives, paints, cosmetics, and printing products, as well as in some candies and soft drinks. Gum arabic can also be found in shoe polish, the glue on postage stamps, ceramic glazes, and even cigarette papers. Cheaper alternatives are becoming more widely available; however, gum arabic remains a useful ingredient. Sudan is the world's largest exporter of gum arabic, providing between 75 and 80 percent of global output. As many as five million people are thought to depend on the harvesting of gum arabic for their livelihoods.

economic situation. The infrastructure is greatly neglected, and foreign investment has declined. Furthermore, the US has imposed several rounds of sanctions on Sudan.

Sudan continues to seek revenues to replace the oil industry. Mining, some manufacturing, and gum arabic exports are key industries. Agriculture provides employment for 80 percent of the work force. The country remains one of the least developed in the world, with 46.5 percent of the population living below the poverty level.

FARMING

Sudan has the potential to become a major producer of cash crops but suffers from the ups and downs of world prices. Sudan has a total land area of about

460 million acres (186 million ha). According to the Sudanese government, 20 percent of that is potentially prime agricultural land, but only about 17 million acres (6.9 million ha) are under active cultivation. Agriculture is the main source of livelihood for 80 percent of the population. Cotton provides the third-largest export earnings, after gold and the production of oil.

Sorghum is an important crop in Sudan because it is so drought resistant.

The most fertile region is near Khartoum, between the White and Blue Niles. There the land is rich in agricultural and grazing properties. Because of this, it is called "the granary of the Sudan."

The area south of Khartoum is a major cotton-growing area. Cotton is an important crop for Sudan. It grows well in the hot, dry climate around Khartoum but needs constant irrigation. It is harvested largely by hand, then separated from the seed cases in the local cotton-ginning plants. Sudan has also been cultivating a variety of extra-fine cotton that is highly resistant to diseases. The cotton industry was nationalized in 1970, and cotton is sold and exported through the Cotton Marketing Board. However, cotton production has dropped sharply in recent years, with only 4,700 tons (4,263 metric tons) exported in 2014, compared to 31,800 tons (28,848 metric tons) in 2013. The decline has been attributed to the failure of the 2005 El Gezira scheme, a major project aimed at developing and improving industrial farming techniques. The scheme failed in part due to its inability to adapt to fluctuating world agriculture markets. Cotton production is expected to rebound to its former successful levels.

Sorghum is another very successful crop in Sudan. It is a drought-resistant grain and has been the staple food of most of Africa for centuries. Besides being an important food crop for the country, it is also an export crop. The sorghum plant grows about 13 feet (4 m) tall and bears a large flower head

Here, workers construct an oil pipeline.

on which round seeds form. The seeds are ground into flour and made into porridge and flatbread; both are staple foods in Sudan. Sorghum can also be brewed into beer. Another important grain for the local market is rice. Sesame is also a growing export industry. Other crops include sugarcane, peanuts, onions, and sunflower seeds.

ANIMAL HUSBANDRY

In vast areas of eastern and western Sudan, nomads roam with their herds, moving from one oasis to another, cropping the land as they go. The animals are mostly cattle, camels, sheep, and goats.

More than any other section of the economy, the tending of livestock has suffered from the years of drought, famine, and war. The drought brought the herders to the cities to find water, and thousands of the animals died in the long journeys. As animals died, the people who depended on them set up shantytowns around the cities or came to depend more and more on refugee camps. In the South, where there was no drought, animals were taken by raiding troops from both sides of the war and even killed as part of a scorched-earth policy to stop southern soldiers from finding food. Now that the war in the South is over, livestock production has proved its vast potential by becoming an important contributor to the agricultural economy. By 2009, livestock and related products made up nearly half of all agricultural exports.

Nomadic herders graze their cattle through much of Sudan.

THE WOODS AND RIVERS

Sudan has 173 million acres (70 million ha) of forest area, which is entirely owned by the government. Between 1990 and 2005, 21.8 million acres (8.8 million ha), or about 13 percent, of the forest was logged for firewood. Other forestry products include beeswax, tannin, senna, charcoal, and luxury woods such as mahogany.

Fishing on the Nile is an important local industry, but the fisheries are barely exploited. Nile perch are readily caught from the banks and provide daily food and most of the protein for people living along the river. Dried fish are traded with nomads for milk and other animal products. A fishing industry has also been encouraged along the Red Sea coast.

GETTING AROUND SUDAN

Sudan has an estimated 7,394 miles (11,900 km) of roads but only 2,684 miles (4,320 km) of paved roads. Most people travel on the back of open trucks; often sixty people are crushed into a space in which twenty people would be cramped. Trucks travel across packed-earth tracks that become swamps when it rains and extremely rough when it is dry. Many roads are impassable in the wet season. The roads in Sudan continue to undergo expansion, especially between Khartoum and the Red Sea. However, most rural areas of the country remain inaccessible by wheeled transport.

Passenger trains link some of Sudan's major cities.

Sudan has about 2,486 miles (4,000 km) of navigable waterways on the Nile and its tributaries, although only 1,056 miles (1,700 km) are navigable throughout the year. South of Khartoum, the Nile is navigable into South Sudan. There are two passenger ferry services in northern Sudan, one coming weekly, traveling between Wadi Halfa and Aswan, Egypt. The other runs across the Red Sea between Jeddah, Saudi Arabia, and Port Sudan.

There are currently six registered air carriers within Sudan. Since 2012, the national carrier Sudan Airways has been owned by the Sudanese government. It has a fleet of just four aircraft and has been banned from operating within the European Union since 2010. Based in Khartoum, Sudan Airways serves six domestic and eight international destinations. Sudan has approximately seventy-four airports, but only sixteen have paved runways. Important airports in Sudan include Khartoum International Airport, Port Sudan, El Obeid, and Al Fashir.

The government-owned Sudan Railways operates the country's limited rail system. It serves mainly the more populous northern and central regions. The main line runs from Wadi Halfa to Khartoum and southwest to El Obeid. It also passes to Nyala in southern Darfur and Waw in South Sudan. The rail connects Atbarah and Sannar with Port Sudan, and Sannar with Ad-Damazin, in addition to providing an 870-mile (1,400 km) line to the cotton-growing region of El Gezira.

INDUSTRY

Before the exportation of oil, most industry in Sudan consisted of food-processing plants around Khartoum, particularly plants processing cottonseed and peanut oil, wheat flour, raw sugar, and gum arabic. There are also factories producing cement, cotton textiles, glass, paper, and light machinery.

During the 1970s, the government nationalized most industries and confiscated several foreign-owned firms, but this policy was reversed in the 1980s, and foreign investment was again encouraged. The introduction of Islamic law in 1983, which made it illegal to lend money at interest, confused the issue again. Large-scale industrial growth is also constrained by the underdeveloped and expensive transportation system, the inadequate infrastructure, and the lack of skilled manpower.

Although Sudan has many airports, only a few have paved runways.

One industry that helped Sudan boost its export earnings is oil. Oil was discovered in the early 1980s in the South but was not exploited until the late 1990s because of rebel activity. In August 1999, the government launched the strategically important 994-mile (1,600 km) pipeline that connects the Heglig oil field to a refinery on the Red Sea near Port Sudan. In 2003, the pipeline was extended another 373 miles (600 km), and oil production reached an estimated three hundred thousand barrels a day. Out of those, two hundred thousand barrels were exported, and about seventy thousand barrels were consumed locally. Most of the petroleum is exported as crude, although some petroleum is refined for the local market. Additional pipelines were planned, but construction slowed after South Sudan's independence in 2011. South Sudan was home to three-quarters of the oil production. However, since much of the pipeline infrastructure is based in Sudan, the two countries hope to work together.

Sudan aims to develop its medical industry, with the intent of becoming an East African hub for the production of medicines and medical equipment.

MINERALS

Sudan has considerable natural resources of gold, iron ore, copper, zinc, tungsten, chromium, manganese, magnetite, salt, and mica, but because of

Sudan is rich in minerals, such as gold. Many miners search for gold each day.

political instability and difficult terrain, very little exploration or large-scale mining had been carried out until quite recently. Gold has been mined for centuries in northern Sudan and the Red Sea Hills. The western region has vast untapped reserves of uranium. Chromite, a black ore from which chromium is extracted, exists near the Ethiopian border.

In 2012, President al-Bashir opened Sudan's first gold refinery, one of the largest in Africa. Gold quickly replaced oil as Sudan's leading export commodity. In 2009, 4 tons (3.6 metric tons) of gold were produced; by 2014, this had increased to 36 tons (33 metric tons), with an expected 74 tons (67 metric tons) in 2015. In 2016, the country expected to produce 100 tons (90.7 metric tons) of gold, making it Africa's second-largest gold producer. With this level of continued growth, Sudan seems likely to soon be one of the world's top-ten gold producers.

POWER

In 2014, Sudan's total installed electrical production was an estimated 12 billion kilowatt hours. Access to electricity throughout Sudan is limited. Only 35 percent of the population have access to electricity. Sixty-three percent of urban areas have been given electricity, compared to 21 percent of rural areas. Most towns have electricity for only a few hours a day. Outside of towns, electricity comes from small, individually owned gasoline-driven generators.

While Sudan has seen some success with hydroelectric power facilities, much of the country's energy still comes from fossil fuels. There is enormous potential for self-sufficiency and the development of renewable resources, including opportunities for further hydroelectric, wind, and solar power generation, but so far the government has had difficulty getting sufficient financing.

One hydroelectric construction set to better meet Sudan's electrical needs is the Merowe Dam Project. Located just below the Fourth Cataract at Merowe, this hydroelectric project, budgeted at about $1.2 billion, has the capacity to generate 1,250 megawatts of power to Khartoum, Port Sudan, Dongola, and Atbara. The project opened in 2009.

Meanwhile, in 2008 Sudan became a member of the Regional Center for Renewable Energy and Energy Efficiency (RCREEE). The country has stated its goal that by 2031, 11 percent of its electricity generation will come from renewable sources excluding hydropower.

INTERNET LINKS

https://www.iea.org/countries/non-membercountries/sudan
This website gives information about Sudan's oil, coal, and renewable energy resources.

http://www.sudanembassy.org/index.php/transportation-services
The Sudanese Embassy offers an overview of current air, land, and train travel services in Sudan.

http://data.un.org/CountryProfile.aspx?crName=SUDAN#Trade
Download reports and data on Sudanese imports and exports here.

ENVIRONMENT

A fertile area on the banks of the Nile

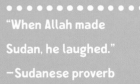

5

• • • • • • • • • • • • • •

"When Allah made
Sudan, he laughed."
—Sudanese proverb

SUDAN'S GEOGRAPHIC DIVERSITY has meant that historically it has been a land of natural riches. Within the country's boundaries are the fertile farmlands of the Nile watershed, open savannas teeming with an abundance of wildlife, and below the ground, precious minerals waiting to be mined. However, two civil wars and decades of corruption have taken their toll. Now the country is suffering from worsening environmental problems.

While Sudan is still home to an impressive variety of wildlife, the once thriving animal populations have become the victims of widespread hunting and few regulatory protections. Meanwhile, recurrent droughts, lack of clean water, and desertification are driving population migration, in turn leading to social conflicts. Foreign aid agencies are attempting to implement programs that will protect both the Sudanese people and their habitat, but progress is slow, with many obstacles to be overcome.

ANIMAL LIFE

Sudan hosts a variety of wildlife. Out of thirteen mammalian orders in Africa, twelve can be found living in Sudan. Because of its varied wildlife, Sudan generates significant revenue through tourism and sport hunting.

Before the outbreak of the civil war, Sudan was known among African countries as the region with the most abundant game and wildlife tourism. Popular stretches for hunting are in the area between the Red Sea Hills and the Nubian Desert. From October to February, game such as the Nubian ibex, the Eritrean and Sommering gazelle, and the baboon are hunted. In the western desert, the hunting season lasts from September through February, with addaxes, Barbary sheep, red-fronted gazelles, ostriches, and white oryx being hunted. Birds such as ducks, bustards, guinea fowls, and doves are hunted from October to January.

For Sudan, the economic value of allowing sport hunting far outweighs its environmental drawbacks, as sport hunting brings in millions of dollars in local income. However, the main causes of extinction of wild animals in Sudan are the country's inability to sustain the reproduction of its hunted wildlife and the lack of oversight of hunting, leading to decimation of many populations. As of 2015, the United Nations reports that 123 species in Sudan are listed as threatened. Sudan has also often been accused of blatant attempts to poach endangered species such as elephants and rhinos to promote an illegal ivory trade regardless of the international ban in 1989. In February 2005, an international conservation group allegedly discovered more than eleven thousand ivory trinkets, ranging from pendants to cigarette holders, openly on sale in Khartoum.

Sudan contends that some wildlife is destructive to humans and their livestock, crops, and property. A species of bird called the red-billed queleas has been destroying cereal crops, costing Sudan millions in potential revenue annually. Sudan's drilling for oil and the construction of oil pipelines in the South have also caused the fragmentation and loss of habitats.

Sudan's struggling economy and uncertain political climate have made the implementation of any major conservation initiatives rather difficult. Sudan has made efforts in preservation by designating about 14,277 square miles (36,979 sq km) of national parks and game reserves for wildlife protection. More was originally designated but is now part of South Sudan. Nevertheless, this amount of protected land is less than 2 percent of Sudan's total land area.

The independence of South Sudan in 2011 saw the loss of most of Sudan's national parks and game reserves. Parks such as Bandingilo and Boma were now part of Sudan's new neighbor, leaving few protected lands within the nation. Those parks that did remain had been largely neglected during years of war. Few resources were dedicated to providing any environmental management, and so illegal forestry for the charcoal trade and unregulated hunting caused widespread damage. However, postwar Sudan has been working with international agencies in an attempt to rehabilitate some of its parks.

A flock of white pelicans in Dinder National Park

Sudan's largest national park is Dinder. Established in 1935, the park covers 2,750 square miles (7,123 sq km) in southeastern Sudan. Dinder is home to more than 150 species of birds and 27 large mammals, including leopards and cheetahs. Lions were discovered in the park in 2016. Much of the park is under threat from nomadic cattle herders, and populations of deer and antelope have suffered with the encroachment of these outsiders. Elsewhere in Sudan, the Suakin Archipelago has been proposed as a national park, although its status has not yet been verified. The group of islands is located in the Red Sea. Popular with divers, they are home to coral reefs, 4 species of turtle, and breeding colonies of 5 types of bird. If protected, this would be Sudan's second protected marine area. The first, Sanganeb Atoll Marine Park is a coral island where more than 300 species of fish can be found.

Sudan also has numerous environmental bodies to ensure some degree of conservation and preservation of wildlife. A leading nongovernmental organization is the Sudanese Environment Conservation Society (SECS), established in 1975, with approximately one hundred branches throughout Sudan. Aside from SECS, the Higher Council of the Environment and Natural Resources ensures that the appropriate authorities follow up on long-term plans for conservation and a sustainable use of natural resources. Other environmental bodies include the Wildlife Research Center, the Wildlife and Environment Conservation Administration, the National Center for Research, the Remote Sensing Authority, and the Plan Sudan Organization. Universities in Sudan also play important roles in promoting environmental conservation and awareness.

Khartoum University helps promote environmental awareness.

CLEAN WATER

Although 72 percent of Sudan lies within the basin of the Nile and its tributaries, the people of Sudan struggle to have an adequate supply of potable water. For years the civil wars hindered the building of a proper infrastructure for water and sanitation. Schools and hospitals often have to make do with inadequate facilities. Two-thirds of urban populations in Sudan have access to improved drinking water, compared with 50 percent of rural populations. However, compared with 43.9 percent of urban dwellers, only 13.4 percent of the rural population has access to adequate sanitation facilities, such as a connection to a sewer or a septic tank system or even a simple pit latrine. Often there are no toilets or modern water facilities in schools, and schoolchildren usually have to carry their own supply of water from home and perform bodily functions in areas surrounding the schools.

The return of more than two million people displaced by civil war and other ongoing conflicts has served to worsen the water issue, as more people fight for the limited access to water and sanitation in areas where such resources are already very limited. The problem is compounded

Women collect water from a well in the desert.

by drought and the discharge of silt from dams. The silt ends up blocking the Nile water currents, decreasing the volume of water flow and making Sudanese rivers open to invasion of weeds and waterborne diseases. The neglected infrastructure of the rainwater drainage system has also given rise to incidences of malaria, especially during the rainy season.

Aside from the threat to human health, inadequate access to safe water and sanitation will inhibit agriculture and animal husbandry and degrade the land with sewage. In Darfur, inadequate water and appalling sanitation conditions, where raw sewage mingled with water sources, have resulted in outbreaks of cholera and diarrhea. Furthermore, what few wells and water systems exist in Darfur are either in disrepair or made inoperable by the ongoing conflict. Lack of reliable data is compounded by a lack of staff skilled in the operation and management of a reliable water infrastructure.

To address the issue in Darfur, a drilling rig was purchased to provide potable water for the internally displaced. Plans are in place to install new hand pumps and water tanks to accommodate more than two million people. The Sustainable Community Water Management Committee has also been formed, boring more than forty holes to provide water for the general population in Sudan. Another initiative to improve access to sustainable safe water, the Water for Recovery and Peace Program (WRAPP), was in operation from 2004 to 2008 with emphasis on the Bahr al-Ghazal, Nuba Mountains, Upper Nile, and South Blue Nile regions. The program's goal was to improve access to a safe water supply, while also raising awareness about sanitation and hygiene. During the program's four-year run, it implemented more than seven hundred new boreholes, rehabilitated a further five hundred boreholes, and constructed public toilet blocks. All in all, it is thought that the projects benefited 1.4 million Sudanese. Under the School Sanitation and Hygiene Education (SSHE) Project, UNICEF, together with the Ministry of Education and the National Water Corporation, successfully provided some school areas with water supplies, sanitation facilities, and hygiene education.

A GROWING DESERT

Some of the main causes of deforestation in Sudan, leading to desertification, are the harvesting of firewood, the overgrazing of animals, and drought. Between 2000 and 2005, Sudan lost its forest land at an average rate of 1.45 million acres (589,000 ha) per year. Over the course of a decade, 12 million acres (4.8 million ha) of fertile land became desert. Since South Sudan gained independence in 2011, the problem has worsened. Now only 10 percent of Sudan's land is under forest cover. Darfur particularly is experiencing major deforestation. The population's dependence on wood and charcoal for its cooking needs has led to strong competition for scarce natural resources. Approximately 60 percent of Darfur's population depends on wood, going through 3,700 square miles (9,583 sq km) of forests annually. The deforestation problem is so severe that some people have resorted to digging under the earth for roots.

Grasslands cover approximately 80 percent, or 575,000 square miles (1,489,000 sq km), of Sudan. Unfortunately, agricultural mismanagement has led to rampant overgrazing and the disappearance of several grasses and herbs, including *Blepharis linariifolia* and *Cadaba farinosa* in many areas. As more areas are expanded to accommodate agricultural developments such as irrigation schemes and rainland crops, areas available to nomads for grazing will become even more limited. Yet the demand for meat, cheese, and milk is greater than ever with the increasing number of refugees. This demand has led to an explosion in livestock figures. In 1990, Sudan was home to an estimated 27 million livestock (primarily cattle, sheep, goats, and camels). This number is now thought to be as high as 135 million. With the extreme increase comes a need for more grazing land. As a result, huge swathes of land face long-term damage from overgrazing.

There has been little reforestation effort, as awareness is weak among the majority of the public and the policymakers. The civil war also made reforestation difficult due to differing environmental policies. Despite the rapid rate of deforestation in Sudan, reforestation efforts have been few, due largely to lack of education, war, and drought. Deforestation affects not only people's potential means of livelihood, as poor soil conditions cannot sustain crops, but also wildlife by destroying their habitats. One successful reforestation program is in Kassala, near the Sudan-Eritrea border. There, refugees have planted more than nineteen million trees in a United Nations High Commissioner for Refugees (UNHCR) program. Over the past twenty-five years, the result has been the transformation of 70,177 acres (28,400 ha) of land into fertile farmland. The land provides food for the local population and grazing land, while also providing protection against further erosion and land loss.

Several forest legislations have been issued, although the infrastructure for enforcing these laws is lacking. A lot of planning is needed to sustain healthy forest biodiversity. Improper land use has been identified, and the government has appointed the Forests National Corporation (FNC) to provide a balanced supply of forest goods and services to the population. Attempts at reforestation include planting trees as windbreaks around villages in the North, encouraging seedling nurseries, and promoting the growing of fruit-tree orchards in the South. Sudan's National Action Plan to Combat

Charcoal is widely sold to use when cooking.

Desertification (SNAP) is left in charge to cover the problem of desertification for most of the land's desert or semidesert regions. International agencies have also helped by curbing the population's excessive need for firewood. They introduced the fuel-efficient stove program, in which stoves made from water, mud, and donkey dung reduce the need for firewood by 50 percent.

LACK OF RAIN

One of the major obstacles to Sudan's securing a permanent livelihood from agriculture and livestock is that the country suffers from periodic droughts. Sudan's low rainfall, as little as 2.4 inches (60 millimeters) in some areas, has severely hurt agricultural production and depleted water resources. Since the infamous drought of 1985—1986 that brought famine to the land, Sudan has been at the mercy of the weather, with droughts in 1989, 1990, 1997, and 2000 as well. In 2011, what has been called the worst drought for sixty years struck much of East Africa, including Sudan. Further drought conditions have continued to take their toll in 2015 and 2016. Each time, crops fail, and livestock and land for pasture are lost. This is because many of Sudan's water yards and water pumps are nonfunctional. Desertification, already a problem, has been exacerbated by the droughts.

Droughts destabilize the population and break down traditional agricultural and livestock practices. Kordofan in western Sudan, the Darfur regions, and parts of central Sudan are usually the worst hit. Although all the causes of such extreme weather conditions are not clear, some scientists have pointed to deforestation and global warming as a few of the main causes.

While it may be possible for Sudan to combat regional desertification, the causes of global warming are largely international. Sudan, for its part, has signed and ratified several climate-change protocols aimed at reducing and releasing only acceptable levels of greenhouse gases into the atmosphere. The government has also made the best of this difficult situation by improving data-collection and early-warning systems in the Red Sea region. This facilitates a quick-response system on modes of assistance when the next drought strikes. Other measures to reduce the effects of drought include upgrading water-harvesting techniques and educating rural communities on how to save their supplies for the days when there is no rain. The Turra water dam project is one example of conserving and channeling water. Located in North Darfur, the dam's reservoir can store up to 71,937 cubic yards (55,000 cubic m) of water, benefiting about four thousand people, including nomadic herders in the area with their eight thousand goats, four hundred sheep, one thousand camels, six thousand donkeys, and one hundred horses.

Drought has affected much of Sudan, leaving the earth dry and cracked.

INTERNET LINKS

http://reliefweb.int/sites/reliefweb.int/files/resources/Sudan_WASH_Sector%20final.pdf
This fact sheet from Reliefweb provides information about sanitation and access to clean water in Sudan.

http://www.secs.org.sd
This national NGO has been dedicated to environmental conservation since 1975. Projects have included water conservation, natural resource management, and reforestation.

http://web.unep.org/disastersandconflicts
This website gives links to a number of reports on post—civil war Sudan, including reports on desertification and wildlife protection.

SUDANESE

A nomadic family moves to a new location.

6

The *taqia* is a short, rounded cap worn by many Sudanese men. It can be worn on its own or with a turban wrapped around it.

SUDAN IS A COUNTRY WITH GREAT diversity among its peoples. In fact, some say it is one of the most diverse places on the African continent. Historically, Sudan has been a meeting point between Arabian and African cultures, and that is still evident today. The majority of peoples in the North and in the Khartoum area consider themselves of Arab descent. Their manner of clothing follows Muslim traditions. Their buildings reflect the civilizations that once lived here—walled courtyards and remnants of Nubian and Egyptian cultures.

Further east and to the south are more of the many individual tribal groups. Some have adopted Arabic habits; others are proud of their Nilotic African traditions. In appearance, they look much more African than some of their northern neighbors. Clothing and religious habits also vary, although these are, to some extent, becoming more influenced by Sudan's adoption of sharia law.

THE NORTHERN PEOPLES

Around 70 percent of Sudanese people are considered Sudanese Arabs, and most of these speak Arabic and live an Arabic lifestyle. Some of those who call themselves Arabs are descendants of Arabs who immigrated to Sudan, while others belong to Sudanese groups who fully adopted Arabic language and culture. The Arabs live chiefly in northern Sudan, in settled communities and extended families rather than in nomadic groups. They consider the home a very private place, but they are also very hospitable and freely offer strangers a rest and a meal. Arab people fill all walks of life in Sudan, from small farmers to city intellectuals. Main Arab tribes in Sudan include the Ja'alayin, the Juhayna, and the Shagia. The Juhayna are nomadic, while the Ja'alayin are agriculturalists. The Juhayna have two subgroups, the Kabbabish and the Baggara. The Shagia are partly nomadic and partly agriculturists. Although they originally lived only in northern Sudan, today they can be found throughout the country.

The other major group in northern Sudan is the Nubian peoples, who represent around 8 percent of the population of Sudan. They speak Nubian, an ancient language with its own alphabet and literature. Modern Nubians also speak Arabic. Many were resettled in other areas of Sudan after the Aswan Dam flooded their land. They are gradually becoming assimilated into Arab culture. In appearance, they are close to their Arab neighbors, with straight black hair and slightly darker skin.

THE WESTERN PEOPLES

Farther to the west are people such as the settled Fur, a Muslim group after whom the Darfur provinces are named; the Baggara tribes, who are nomadic traders; and the Zaghawa, who are also nomads. The Zaghawa regularly make the enormous trek across the desert to the Libyan border. There they sell their great herds of camels and trade in salt, a rare commodity in Sudan. The Fallata people, across Sudan, are unlike any of their neighbors and are thought to have descended from the Fulani group, a Muslim nomadic tribe from northern Nigeria.

The Baggara tribes are nomads who claim Arab descent. By the sixteenth century, nomadic Arabs from northern Africa and Arabia had migrated as far as Lake Chad and had intermarried with Africans. In the eighteenth century, their descendants moved to Sudan, where the land was suited to their nomadic lifestyle.

Traditionally they have a social system based on family ties, changing allegiances, and blood feuds. Power is not hereditary but stems from wealth and strength of personality. Many Baggara groups today live in central Sudan. The major tribes include the Rizeigat, the Ta'isha, and the Habbaniya in Darfur, and the Homr, the Messiria, and the Hawazma in Kordofan.

THE EASTERN PEOPLES

The Rashaida are a nomadic tribe of people who arrived in the Sudan region from Saudi Arabia in the early nineteenth century. They are thought to be related to the Bedouin peoples. They live in goatskin tents in the area around Kassala, in northeastern Sudan, and in the neighboring country of Eritrea. They are easily recognizable by the heavy veils and silver jewelry worn by the women and the colorful turbans worn by the men.

When a girl from the Rashaida tribe is ready to marry, she approaches the man she wants and flirtatiously lifts her veil so that he can see her chin. If he accepts her offer, he must find one hundred camels for her bride price. By tradition, the Rashaida breed camels and goats, but in modern times many of them drive Toyota trucks.

The Beja are Muslims living in the Red Sea Hills. They became famous in Britain in the nineteenth century for their fierce fighting in the Mahdist battles. Although they are traditionally nomadic, some Beja have adopted a lifestyle of farming cotton. They regard the sea as hostile and do not eat fish except in times of extreme need. The major Beja groups are the Bisharin, the Hadendowa, the Amarar, the Ababda, and the Beni Amer. Their thick, curly hair gives them quite a distinctive appearance, and those who work on the docks in Port Sudan are distinguishable by their traditional hairstyles. The Beja speak both Sudanese Arabic and their own Beja language.

Three Rashaida children. The older girl wears the veil traditionally worn by the tribe's women.

In 1952, the Beja formed the Beja Congress, a political party aimed at giving them more regional autonomy. From 1999 to 2003, they repeatedly sabotaged construction of the pipeline that ran through their lands to Port Sudan, and they formed an alliance with the Sudan Liberation Movement. A peace treaty with the Sudanese government was later signed, but after the 2010 election, where they failed to win a single seat, they withdrew from the peace treaty and have since realigned themselves with the Sudan Liberation Movement.

THE SOUTHERN PEOPLES

Sudan's southern regions are home to many of the country's almost six hundred individual tribal groups, and as such, there is enormous cultural and linguistic diversity. Much of this diversity remains, even after the 2011 independence of what is now South Sudan.

Since 2011, South and North Kordofan make up southern and south-central Sudan. The region is home to both Arab tribes, such as the Bedairiah, Dar Hamid, and Kawahla, as well as some of the Nilotic peoples, including the Nuba, Shilluk, and Dinka.

The Dinka were once the largest non-Arab ethnic group in southern Sudan, making up 20 percent of the southern population. They are traditional nomadic herders whose lives revolve around their animals. Fiercely independent, they saw the introduction of sharia law as an attack on their way of life. While many of them try to live peacefully, many more became soldiers of the SPLA, living deep in the southern forests, raiding other ethnic groups for food, shelter, and clothes, and threatening all road and air transport. Most of their rebel activities came to a halt, however, when the SPLA successfully brokered a deal with the government in 2005, giving the people significant regional autonomy and exempting them from sharia law. Many of the Dinka are now in South Sudan, but some remain in the Kordofan regions.

Likewise, the Shilluk are now primarily in South Sudan, but some remain north of the new border. They are an animist group who have farmed the fertile banks of the Nile south of Khartoum since the sixteenth century.

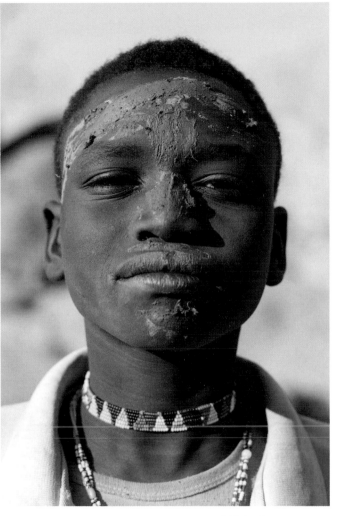

A Nuba boy

The mountains of southern Kordofan are home to the Nuba, a dark-skinned group of tribes, some of whom are Muslim. Exact population numbers vary, but 2003 figures estimated a Nuba population of 1.07 million. The Nuba people inhabit the Nuba Mountains in Kordofan. For centuries, the fifty groups that make up the Nuba lived peacefully among themselves and with their Arab neighbors. They kept cattle and terraced the mountainsides to grow grain, vegetables, and fruit. Many of them practiced an unconventional form of Islam that allowed alcohol and pork, but there were sometimes Christians and animists within the same family. They went for the most part naked.

REFUGEES

The second civil war in Sudan killed nearly two million people and displaced four million more. Some of those displaced have since left for Chad and Egypt, while others have gone to Asia and Europe. The ongoing conflict in Darfur has displaced even more Sudanese. In Kalma, Darfur's biggest refugee camp, more than 150,000 people are dependent on food aid.

Refugee camps in central and southern Sudan are filled with Sudanese people displaced by the war, as well as with refugees from Chad, Uganda, and other African countries.

During the 1970s and 1980s, many tourists came to the area to see their traditional dances and wrestling. The government began a campaign to clothe the Nuba and force them to follow traditional Islamic rules. After several years of persecution, the Nuba declared their support for the SPLA, and since then the policy of "civilizing" the Nuba has given way to eradication. The Nuba Mountains have been cut off from the rest of the world, and government troops have carried out a scorched-earth policy, killing and burning the Nuba's crops and animals. Whole groups have been forced into camps where men and women are segregated, and there have been reports of rape and genocide.

By 1999, more than one hundred thousand Nuba had been displaced. The signing of the Burgenstock Agreement in 2002 calling for a cease-fire in the Nuba Mountains between the government and the SPLA has given the Nuba people some semblance of normality. The peace protocol signed three years later was meant in part to ensure significant autonomy for the people. Violence against the Nuba people has resumed since 2011 and continues as of 2016.

CLOTHING

Clothing style varies whether one lives in the city or in the country. In cities, business is conducted in Western or Arab dress, usually a thin short-sleeve shirt and cotton trousers for men and a light cotton dress with a *tobe* (TOH-bay) for women. A tobe is a 10-yard (9 m) piece of thin fabric. It is wrapped around and around the body, covering its outlines and leaving only the face exposed. Men wear ties and jackets on formal occasions.

At home and on the streets, men from the North relax in the loose, long cotton shirt called a *jallabiya* (CHAL-a-bee-ah), loose pants, and a turban called an *imma* (EM-ah). They are also likely to wear this dress for formal occasions.

Inside the house, many northern women wear Western clothes that are longer and cover more of the body than their Western peers might want to wear in such a climate. Out of the house, they cover this with a tobe. A tobe's color is chosen to match the clothes underneath. For work, a white tobe is worn, while women in eastern Sudan often wear a black tobe. In some areas in the West and North, the tobes are very colorful.

A man wearing traditional Sudanese clothing travels in a cart guided by a donkey.

BODY DECORATION

Scarring is a very ancient tradition in Sudan. Frescoes in the historical city of Meroë depict scarring patterns on the faces of people. Scarification is a major ethnic and aesthetic component not only among the southern people in Sudan but also across other parts of Africa. Sometimes scarification is performed on girls to mark the stages of life, such as puberty or marriage. Men also have facial scarring, which is carried out as part of their initiation into manhood.

A common scarring pattern among the Shilluk is a row of raised bumps across the forehead, made by rubbing ash into the wounds. The Shilluk king has this type of scarring. The Nuer have six parallel lines on their foreheads, while the Ja'alayin have lines marked on their cheeks. The scarring is, to them, considered beautiful and identifies ethnicities.

Thorns and razor blades are used to remove skin, creating the sholouk, *or "facial cuts." Many medical organizations are concerned about the dangers of disease, especially HIV and hepatitis, which might be transmitted through the use of unclean tools and unsafe healing methods. The practice is not as common as it once was, although in many rural areas, social and family pressures remain strong.*

Other forms of body decoration include lip tattooing, practiced by some women in the North, and painting hands and feet with intricate henna patterns.

Women can be arrested for appearing in public dressed immodestly. This law becomes more relaxed the farther south one travels. Traditionally, the southern people wear little except jewelry. Some (particularly older women) wear beaded aprons or sarongs, and practice facial scarring. However, both the near-nudity and the facial scarring are in rapid decline, particularly as Islamic laws and traditions spread.

Although the 2005 interim constitution allows for freedom of religion, President al-Bashir has publicly stated that he views Sudan as a strictly Islamic country, with no room for diversity. The increasing imposition of sharia law can be seen throughout Sudan. In 2015, a group of Christian women were arrested in front of a church in Khartoum. They were charged with breaking indecency laws by wearing skirts and trousers in public. Some of the women were found guilty but were spared the traditional punishment of forty lashes. The women were all originally from the Nuba region. Human rights groups have estimated that as many as forty thousand women each year are arrested and flogged because of their clothing.

Because of government campaigns and the influence of missionaries, many southern people now wear clothes. The government policy of clothing the southern people became part of the conflict between the North and the South. Southerners resent the attempts to impose Islamic laws and customs on their traditional lifestyles, while the people of the North believe that it is their religious duty to encourage the spread of Islam.

A group of Sudanese children

INTERNET LINKS

http://www.genderacrossborders.com/2011/10/27/pain-for-beauty-the-dilemma-of-facial-cutting-in-sudan
This article discusses the practice of facial cutting and scarification rituals in Sudan and how attitudes are changing.

http://nationalclothing.org/35-nationalclothing/africa/sudan/49-national-dress-of-sudan-men-prefer-loose-fitting-robes-and-women-use-wrap-around-cloths.html
Easily understood information and images explain traditional clothing items.

http://www.sudanembassy.org/index.php/tribal-composition
Information on the Sudanese Embassy page details the current ethnic makeup of Sudan's population and the various tribes of each region.

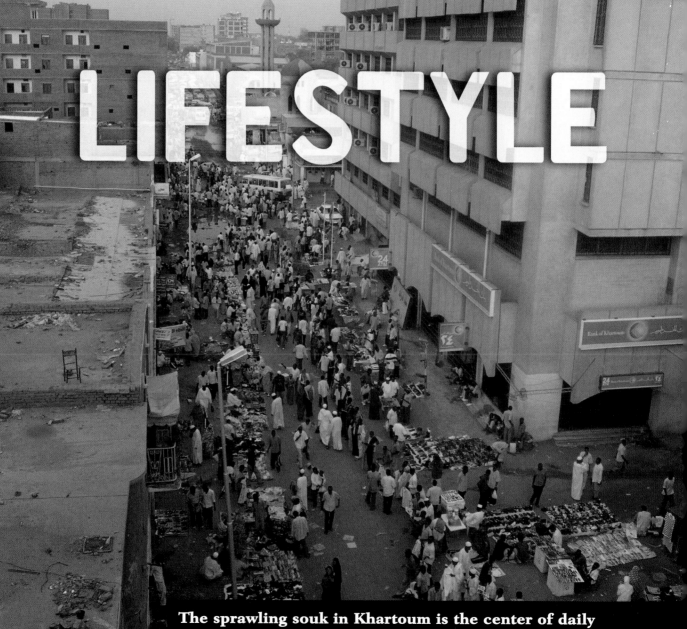

LIFESTYLE

The sprawling souk in Khartoum is the center of daily life for many locals.

N O ONE IN SUDAN HAS ESCAPED THE atrocities of decades of civil war. Even though the civil war has ended, life in Sudan remains uncertain, subject to political unrest, economic ups and downs, famine, ongoing regional conflicts, and the increasingly widespread imposition of sharia law. In many respects, the nomadic peoples have been hardest hit. Drought, famine, and desertification continue to make their way of life more difficult.

But life goes on across Sudan. Despite the struggles and risks, babies are still born, children grow up, and family life continues. The Sudanese are a resilient people who hold on to traditions and community, despite the hardships.

LIFE IN KHARTOUM

During the long, hot days, life in Sudanese cities is conducted at a slow pace. Many people in Khartoum live in modern Western-style apartment blocks with the ease of electricity and piped water. The city suffers from frequent power cuts, however, so refrigeration and air conditioning are almost nonexistent. Most of the daily life of Khartoum is conducted out in the open, under whatever shade is around. Wooden-frame string beds are pulled out of the house into the courtyard to serve as chairs.

7

One tradition among those living near the Nile is to make an amulet of a fishbone and tie it around a newborn baby's neck for luck.

The hustle and bustle of Khartoum is a stark contrast to more rural areas.

In the city, life revolves around the souk, the city market. The souk is a maze of streets where one can easily become lost; it is also the center of a town's social life. The souk is divided into craft and merchandise sections—all the goldsmiths are in one part of the souk, while all the greengrocers are in another. The goldsmiths make jewelry in the back of the shop to sell at the front. Baskets and leather bags are sold here for daily use. Some souks sell only Western luxury items; others sell camels or donkeys in a separate animal souk. Throughout the souk are tea shops where hot, sweet mint tea can be drunk at one's leisure. These are popular places to meet friends and catch up on news and gossip. The Khartoum area's largest souk is in Omdurman, where craftworkers of all kinds make precious objects out of ivory, ebony, gold, and silver. More ordinary souks contain shops selling fresh food, tobacco, and a few electrical goods. Aside from souks, Sudanese also shop at Afra Mall, Sudan's first shopping mall, which opened in Khartoum in 2004. Covering an area of 53,800 square yards (45,000 sq m), the mall offers a movie theater, a hypermarket, a food court, an internet café, a bowling alley, and an ice rink. Beauty salons and electronics and clothing stores are also featured at the mall. More than twenty thousand people visit the mall each day.

Khartoum's city center has skyscrapers, some big hotels, and stores catering to the small number of tourists who venture this far south. Business hours are usually between 8 a.m. and 2 p.m. Everything closes during the afternoon and reopens again when it is cooler, from 6 p.m. to 8 p.m., Saturday through Thursday, with Friday as the day of rest. On Sunday, Christians are allowed two hours to attend church services should they desire to do so.

In wealthier parts of the city, the houses have high fences with carefully guarded four-wheel-drive cars parked outside. Inside are prize possessions like the television and the DVD player. Wealthy families have several servants, who sleep out in the courtyard while the family sleeps inside.

Northern Sudanese villagers also live an Arab lifestyle, with thick-walled square houses built around a central courtyard. Most villages are on the banks of the Nile or at a few desert oases. Similar to life in the cities, village life occurs mostly outside during the day, in courtyards and at roadside tea shops. People work in the fields, tend their animals, and make goods for sale or barter.

NOMADS

More than one-tenth of the population of Sudan has a seminomadic or nomadic existence. Different nomadic groups have different ways of life. The Rashaida in northeastern Sudan make their tents out of woven goat hair, while the tents of the nearby Hadendowa are made out of palm-fiber mats.

Nomads in northern Sudan make their homes in makeshift sheds.

Many northern tribes herd livestock such as cattle, goats, and camels, and they wander the desert following the sudden rainstorms. After a storm, a patch of desert that has been infertile for years will suddenly blossom and provide a temporary pasture for the vast herds of animals.

Other nomads are traders who make long journeys back and forth across the desert using trucks and, to a lesser extent, camel trains, bartering gold or salt for other goods.

IN THE SOUTH

As one travels farther south, both the countryside and the people change. The indigenous population is African rather than Arab, and their lifestyle has little in common with that of their northern compatriots. People wear fewer clothes, and many decorate their bodies with scars.

The typical square, mud-brick houses give way to groups of round houses with mud walls and thatched straw roofs. The houses are arranged in circles

In southern Sudan, the Nuba people live in round houses of thatched straw.

around a swept, earthen courtyard where most of the village activities take place. Most people in rural Sudan live close to other members of their extended family. After his initiation ceremony, a boy will build his own home within the village compound. Cooking is done over an open fire, as most houses lack electricity. The lack of indoor plumbing means that water is drawn from nearby wells, rivers, or streams. The villages are often surrounded by grass walls to keep children in and wildlife out.

Beyond the houses are small fields irrigated once a year by the Nile floods. In the floodplains, as many as three harvests a year can be made. Most families work to produce their own food and enough to barter for their other needs. Sometimes they sell their produce to middlemen, who often pay the villagers as little as possible. There are few paid jobs except for agricultural workers at harvest time.

Away from the floodplains, people depend on wells for water. The government has drilled many wells and provided a series of irrigation canals. In recent years, because of the drain on Sudan's water resources, wells have had to be drilled deeper and deeper before water could be found.

The civil wars brought huge disruption to the lives of many rural Sudanese, with whole ethnic groups being displaced by raids from both sides. Even the current relative peace is still marred by gun battles between rival clans over cattle, pasture, and water.

FAMILY LIFE

Traditionally, many Sudanese have lived with extended family, in communities with aunts, uncles, and cousins. The lineage is passed through the male line, and many social groups can trace their families for generations. The elders of the family are highly respected.

However, the disruption in the traditional patterns of life in Sudan by war, floods, droughts, and famine has resulted in the breakup of traditional family units. Many men have had to leave their families and go in search of work, leaving Muslim women as head of the household for the first time in their lives. The women, however, have some means of income, through remittances and financial help by the extended family.

Many newlywed Sudanese couples live with the wife's family for the first year of marriage, moving out when they have their first child.

Sons also leave home at a very young age so as not to be a burden to their families. They go to the cities, where they quickly become beggars and thieves, sleeping in the streets and often receiving injuries in accidents. In Khartoum and Nyala, there are programs to rehabilitate such children. They are taught a trade and encouraged to return to their homes.

WOMEN'S ROLES

A family poses outside their home.

Sudanese culture, especially in areas most influenced by Islam, adheres to very strict gender roles. Arab women are carefully guarded by their families. They do not mix socially with men who are not their kin, and they cover themselves with long cloths when they go outside. Women tend to spend much more time in the home, while men take care of business outside the home (including doing the daily shopping). There are few Arab girls living on the streets in Sudan; no matter how poor a family is, it is a tenet of their faith that girls are weak and should be protected, and even very distant cousins will be taken in if they have no other means of support.

A girl is often married as a teenager to a man she might have met only a few times and may never have spoken to privately. Her husband pays a bride price to her parents.

The adoption of the 1998 constitution guaranteeing gender equality and the right of women to economic and political freedom somewhat eased the restrictions placed on women. Today, 130 of the 426 seats in the National Assembly are held by women. However, as strict Islamic law is imposed, it remains to be seen how this might impact women's place in society. In 2012, Sudan received one of the lowest possible rankings for women's rights from

Freedom House, a US aid agency. Sudan is one of the few countries that has not signed the Convention on the Elimination of All Forms of Discrimination Against Women (CEDAW). Because tradition tends to dictate that women should remain in the home, they often lack access to suitable health care. The maternal mortality rate in 2015 was 311 deaths per 100,000 live births.

In more rural areas, particularly in the South, gender roles tend to be a little less strict, with men and women both sharing responsibilities for raising crops or herding cattle. The women work hard in the fields, collecting water, caring for animals, and making goods to sell. The Felata across Sudan believe that women should earn their own living. The girls are independent, and many work, selling sweetmeats in the marketplaces. They wear brightly colored clothes and jewelry. Those who get the opportunity attend school wearing shorts just like the boys in their class.

A woman carries items on her head as she walks.

MEDICINE

For most periods since the early twentieth century, the Sudanese people have suffered from frequent epidemics of diseases such as meningitis, sleeping sickness, and yellow fever. The efforts of the Sudan Medical Service (later the Ministry of Health) and missionary institutions reduced the death rate, but the drought, the civil wars, and the current conflict in Darfur still resulted in reducing life expectancy. War, famine, and disease are the major causes of death, and life expectancy is only sixty-two years for men and sixty-six years for women. Infant mortality is around fifty deaths per thousand live births. Years of war and struggle also mean that the population is very young; the median age is 19.6 years.

The civil war and the conflict in Darfur have diverted much-needed medical resources that would otherwise have gone into preventive health care and

FEMALE CIRCUMCISION

Female circumcision, also known as female genital mutilation (FGM), is widely practiced in Sudan, particularly in the North. This highly controversial procedure is widely condemned by health organizations and women around the world. However, it remains an important cultural tradition for many Sudanese. FGM is often associated with Muslim tribes; however, both Christian and Muslim peoples in some regions follow the tradition. There is no mention of it in the Quran.

UNICEF estimates that nine out of ten Sudanese women between the ages of fifteen and forty-nine have been subjected to FGM. The procedure can take place at any time from a few days after birth to puberty. A razor blade is used to remove parts of the genitalia, driven by the belief that it will make a woman pure and more desirable in marriage. Interestingly, it is usually carried out by older women in the community, who insist that the girls will be cast out from the community if they fail to undergo the procedure. Studies increasingly show that many men are against their daughters being cut in this way. FGM often leads to numerous health problems. In addition to the sanitary risks linked to using a razor blade, many women face recurrent infections and difficulty during childbirth.

UNICEF has been part of a widespread campaign to educate Sudanese about the risks of FGM. As a result of their work in eastern Sudan, it is thought that half of all women are now against the procedure, and that number is increasing.

the training of professionals. Even in this period of rebuilding Sudan, health care remains an afterthought, with far less government attention than other aspects of life and the economy. Many valued medical professionals left Sudan to escape the war and seek employment elsewhere. Some have returned, but numbers are still low. It is estimated that there are only twenty-eight doctors per one hundred thousand people. There are few public hospitals in Sudan. Many closed from lack of resources. Those that remain open struggle to provide services. The government has sold many of their resources for personal profit,

while promoting privatized health care that few can afford. There are roughly eight hospital beds per ten thousand people, but many hospitals now rely on volunteers and donations.

Children receive vaccinations.

In rural areas and the South, medical care is very basic. There is a severe shortage of local doctors, so most medical care is undertaken by foreign aid workers and midwives with very basic training. Sometimes the people in the rural areas depend on folk remedies that are limited in their effectiveness.

Only 66 percent of the population has access to safe water and sanitary facilities. Combined with the scarcity of medicines, many people die of easily preventable diseases such as measles and dysentery. Spending on health care has improved somewhat but is still low—only 8 percent of the country's GDP. However, thanks to efforts by the World Health Organization (WHO), the percentage of children immunized against most major childhood diseases had risen to approximately 85 percent by 2014, a vast improvement from just 2 percent in the early 1980s. Diseases such as malaria, river blindness, hepatitis A, and tuberculosis remain endemic in the Nile Valley.

A traditional Sudanese Muslim wedding lasts about three days. Once it would have lasted up to forty days, but that custom is no longer followed. Before the pair is betrothed, a good deal of bargaining goes on between the families of the bride and the groom, who may be related anyway. The groom must pay a bride price to the bride's father in addition to bestowing a dowry on the bride herself.

As the wedding approaches, her body is oiled and perfumed, and all body hair except that on her head is removed using boiled sugar and lemon juice. Her hands are painted with henna in intricate floral patterns.

The night before the wedding, the groom holds a party in the courtyard. A feast is set out, and men and women sit in separate groups to eat. After the food come speeches and dancing. The men dance first, in swaying, stamping rows. The women dance in groups of two or three, joining and stopping, while the men dance continuously. While the dancing goes on, the groom walks around the groups of people waving a stick and shouting; the others shout back or howl at him.

The ceremony itself is carried out the following day by an imam (Muslim leader) in the presence of the parents. The bride and the groom do not take part. Seven women go down to the Nile and throw food in, returning with water to wash the bride's face. That night the bride's family holds another party. The bride dances for the groom and guests.

SCHOOL

Sudan technically provides eight years of free compulsory education, from ages six to fourteen, but in reality, enforcement of the policy and access to educational facilities varies widely throughout the country. In 2001, only 46 percent of Sudan's children attended during the "compulsory" years, and only 21 percent of eligible secondary-age (fourteen-year-old) students attended school. While education is readily available in the North, with 90 percent

of all children having access, few schools remain in the South or the West. Years of conflict have left few facilities in these regions. Even where there are schools, families are often contending with hunger and a need to find work. Nevertheless, the country's current literacy rate continues to show signs of improvement. The total literacy rate is 75.9 percent, 83 percent for men and 68.6 percent among women. Sudan's weak economy has made improving the educational system difficult. Often the teachers are poorly qualified, and the better ones are lost to better-paying nations. As of 2009, 2.2 percent of the GDP was spent on education.

There are two levels of schools: basic (six to fourteen years old) and secondary (fourteen to seventeen years old). The primary language of instruction is Arabic, although English is offered as a foreign language in grades seven through eleven. The school year runs from July to March. The government decision to make Arabic the official language of instruction has been a controversial one in parts of the South and West, leading to a greater reduction of children attending school.

Children attend a rural school in northern Sudan.

Sudan has more than forty institutions of higher learning and technical training colleges throughout the country, but many of these are centered in Khartoum and other cities.

HUNGER

For much of the twentieth century, the lifestyle of many Sudanese was dominated by the need to find food. Although Sudan is rich in fertile agricultural land and mineral resources, population displacement from the war and recurrent droughts have given rise to widespread malnutrition outside the central Nile region.

In 1984 and 1985, western Sudan around Kordofan and Darfur and eastern Sudan near Kassala experienced unprecedented droughts. Roughly four hundred thousand people from Kordofan came to central Sudan in search of food and water for their animals. Seven million people suffered from malnutrition and came close to starvation, and many died. The problem was made worse by temperatures of 126°F (52°C) and ferocious sandstorms.

Malnutrition and famine are widespread in Darfur.

A second wave of famine, this time caused by the war, hit Sudan in 1989. By this time, a relief infrastructure was in place with various aid agencies supplying food, but both the government and the SPLA caused problems, with neither side wanting the other to receive the aid. Much of the aid went to government troops rather than to the citizens of the North or the South, where around 2.6 million people were in need of emergency aid. In some areas of the South, 60 percent of the people suffered from malnutrition.

In 1998, Sudan was once again in the global news, as it faced another severe famine. The food shortages were caused largely by the ongoing war in the southern parts of the country, and human rights abuses by both the government and rebel groups. Both sides were accused of destroying local farmland and crops, and of stealing what food aid was able to reach the area. Monetary aid was also misused and diverted to the buying of weapons rather than food or medical supplies. In Bahr al-Ghazal, in southwestern Sudan, an estimated seventy thousand people died during the famine.

As the nation struggles to recover from civil war, the ongoing ethnic warfare in the Darfur region sees an estimated 2.7 million people, including 1.8 million children, at risk from malnutrition and requiring food assistance. The ongoing insecurity in the region has deterred farmers from cultivating crops for fear of attacks. To make matters worse, in May 2006 the UN World Food Program decreased food aid to Sudan due to the lack of donor funds. The minimum daily requirement was halved from 2,100 calories to 1,050 calories per person to feed about 350,000 people dying from malnutrition and disease. A decade later, the violence in Darfur continues. To date, some 380,000 refugees have fled to neighboring Chad, and at least 2.7 million people have been displaced. There has been little response from the Sudanese government, other than a promise to dismantle the refugee camps, the only shelter remaining for the millions who have lost their homes.

INTERNET LINKS

https://www.lonelyplanet.com/sudan/khartoum
Lonely Planet lists some of the most popular attractions in Sudan's capital.

https://www.unicef.org/sowc
Here you can read reports covering education, health, nutrition, and other factors affecting children's well-being.

http://www.who.int/countries/sdn/en
Visit this website to read statistics, information, and reports about disease rates, childhood mortality, and other health data in Sudan.

RELIGION

A mosque in Khartoum

8

During Ramadan, Muslims perform the Taraweeh, nightly prayers that recite a chapter of the holy book each night.

AN ESTIMATED 97 PERCENT OF Sudan's population is Muslim, with the remaining 3 percent practicing indigenous religions or Christianity. Christians and followers of other religions are a minority and are sometimes persecuted for their beliefs. Everyone in Sudan must follow sharia law, regardless of their personal religious affiliations.

ISLAM

The word "Islam" means "submission." Muslims believe in the word of God and submit to all his words as handed down by the prophets. Islam acknowledges as prophets several figures out of Christianity and Judaism, including Abraham (Ibrahim), Adam, Noah, Moses, and Jesus. Muslims believe that Jesus is merely one of the prophets who have heard the word of God, rather than the Son of God.

The most recent and revered of the prophets is Muhammad (570 CE—632 CE). His following grew, and after his death most of Arabia converted to Islam. Muhammad's birthplace, Mecca in Saudi Arabia, became the religion's holy city because it was there that the first mosque was built. It is called the Kaaba and contains a black stone believed to have been given to Ibrahim by the archangel Gabriel. God's words were collected by Muhammad into a holy book called the Quran.

THE FIVE PILLARS OF FAITH

Muslims must carry out five acts of faith, namely:

- Shahada *(shah-ha-da)*—the first pillar of Islam, according to which believers must publicly declare that there is no God but Allah and that Muhammad is his prophet, or messenger.
- Solat *(soh-lat)*—in reference to prayers carried out five times a day: at sunrise, noon, midafternoon, sunset, and night.
- Zakat *(zah-kat)*—the giving of alms to the poor.
- Puasa *(pua-sah)*—the act of fasting during the holy month of Ramadan.
- *Hajj*—a pilgrimage to Mecca that is to be made at least once in a Muslim's lifetime.

ISLAMIC PRAYER Muslims make a commitment to pray five times a day. At each of the prayer times, the muezzin calls the faithful to the mosque. Before praying, the devotee removes his or her shoes and holds them in the left hand. The body is carefully washed according to ritual and in a certain order. The devotee faces the direction of Mecca and goes through a ritual of standing, bowing, and sitting, reciting prescribed prayers as he or she does so. The prayers should be carried out in a congregation, but if people cannot attend a mosque, they can say their prayers alone. On Fridays, there are special prayers in all mosques.

RAMADAN Fasting is required of all Muslims during the month of Ramadan. Besides refraining from eating and drinking from dawn to dusk during Ramadan, Muslims must also abstain from smoking and other worldly desires. In addition, if they can afford it, they must feed poor people. The fast can be delayed if one is sick, pregnant, or on a hazardous journey.

MECCA Every Muslim who can afford it is obligated to make the journey to Mecca at least once in his or her lifetime. For thousands of Arab people, that once meant a vast journey of several months across the Libyan and Nubian Deserts in a camel train. The pilgrimage must be made in a state of grace, and strict rules have to be observed. Pilgrims have to be in a state of ritual purity, bathing in a special fluid and wearing a seamless white garment. The pilgrims must not cut their hair or nails, engage in marital relations, or shed blood. Once the pilgrims arrive at Mecca, they have to perform a number of rites in a specific order. The rites include running between the tops of Mount Marwah and Mount Safa seven times and stoning the three pillars at Mina, signifying the devil, with seven consecutive pebbles.

Sharing a meal before dawn is part of the month-long Ramadan ritual.

ISLAMIC LAW Islamic law includes both legal and moral concepts. Many of the rules of Islamic law cannot be put into a legal system and must be a matter of conscience.

The laws of Islam are laid down in the Quran and the Sunna, which is a code of conduct for Muslims to follow, and have been added to by various religious groups over many centuries. They uphold the importance of the family and declare men and women to be equal, except that men are "a degree higher." The Quran forbids infanticide of girls, which was once common among the Arab tribes; allocates a degree of inheritance to girls; and describes the treatment of wives. Women are given the right of divorce in the case of ill treatment, but adultery is proscribed, with a punishment of one hundred lashes. Under Islamic law, men are allowed to marry up to four wives and can divorce any wife at will. Other important laws of Islam forbid eating pork and drinking alcohol.

JIHAD Etymologically, *jihad* means "struggle" or "strive." However, there are many interpretations of the word. It is most commonly interpreted as striving toward spiritual self-perfection. Some interpret it to mean a war waged against the enemies of Islam, though it must be noted that the Quran does not condone the arbitrary use of violence but as a last resort.

ANIMIST RELIGIONS

Animist religions are the most ancient religions practiced in Sudan, particularly in the Nilotic South. Animists believe that the natural objects around them have spiritual power and are able to influence their lives in many ways. Many animist groups worship one particular totem, such as a wild animal, a particular tree, or a river, and will do anything to avoid injuring that entity.

Most animist societies worship their ancestors, believing that the spirits of their ancestors must be carefully looked after because they have the power to bring harm or good to the family. Because each group respects the rights of other groups to worship their own ancestors, the various animist religions have never been in conflict, although people have fought for other reasons.

A *faki*, or traditional healer, uses herbs to treat many illnesses.

Many people also believe in the evil eye: a menacing look or glare from a person with magical powers or the help of a witch that could cause them harm. As such, many people wear amulets to protect themselves from curses, and small babies are kept well away from public view in case someone sees them and puts the evil eye on them.

TRADITIONAL HEALING

The aid groups who have gone to Sudan to help with the refugee crises, famines, and floods recorded some of the local beliefs, especially those concerning medicine. One traditional cure for certain illnesses is to burn the victim with hot nails to drive out the illness, while a cure for malaria is to make forty-four cuts on the patient's body. The Fallata in western Sudan have *faki* (FAY-ki), who are part teachers/scholars and part magicians. For one month each year, the faki collect herbs and roots that they make into spells and potions to cure illnesses or arouse the interest of a potential lover.

CHRISTIANITY IN MODERN SUDAN

Nubia had three Christian kingdoms for centuries before the advent of Islam. However, since the secession of South Sudan in 2011, the nation has increasingly adopted strict Muslim laws, and in much of the country, Christianity and other non-Muslim religions are frowned upon.

INTERNET LINKS

http://www.bbc.co.uk/religion/religions/islam/beliefs/sharia_1.shtml
This BBC article explains sharia law.

http://www.pbs.org/empires/islam/eduk12plan.html
This series of lesson plans accompanies the PBS series about Muslim religion, its origins, and its beliefs.

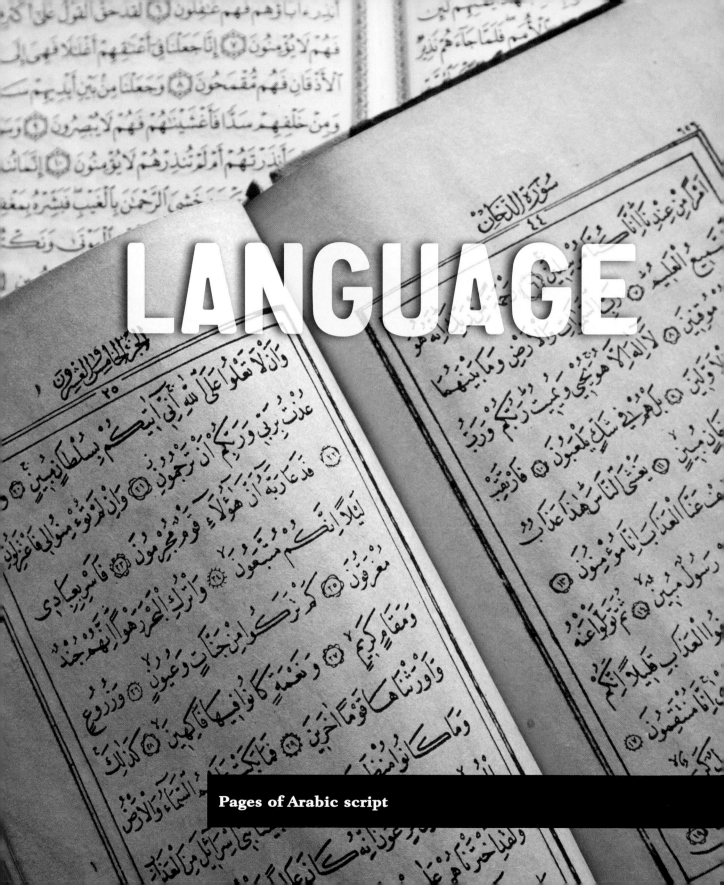

LANGUAGE

Pages of Arabic script

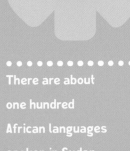

9

. . . .

There are about
one hundred
African languages
spoken in Sudan.

SUDAN'S POPULATION HAS A LARGE diversity of languages. More than one hundred languages and five hundred dialects are spoken in Sudan. Many of these languages are spoken by quite tiny numbers of people.

There are two official languages in Sudan. The main spoken language throughout the country is a Sudanese form of Arabic. Arabic began its rise to prominence in the fourteenth century, and its position was established when it was made the official language of the government of the Funj sheikhdom, the Mahdist state, and early colonial governments. English was designated the country's second official language in the 2005 constitution, which states that both Arabic and English shall be the major languages for government and education. Other key languages include Beja, Tigre, Fur, and some Nubian dialects. Most Sudanese speak at least two or three languages. These include their mother tongue, Arabic, and some English, as well as other local languages.

THE PRIMARY LANGUAGE

Arabic is the major language in Sudan, spoken either as a mother tongue or as a lingua franca among groups of other language speakers. The standard form of Arabic from Saudi Arabia, called Classical Arabic, is the official language and is used in official documents, as well as on formal occasions. However, very few people use it regularly. This causes some educational problems, since it is the official language of education and the language in which textbooks are printed.

GREETINGS AND BODY LANGUAGE

It is common when greeting someone in Arabic to touch one's heart and say, "Is Salaam aleyakum" (Is sah-LAHM ah-LAY-ah-koom; "Peace be with you"), followed by "Kayf halak" (KYFE hah-LAHK) or "Kaefak" (Ka-A-fak; "How are you?").

The right hand is held out in a formal handshake between strangers, although a man will never touch a woman unless the woman offers her hand first. Often men will embrace each other in a hug on greeting, but men and women rarely embrace in this way.

As in many other Muslim countries, use of the left hand is avoided as much as possible. Objects are passed between people with either the right hand or both hands, never the left only. Pointing at someone with the left hand would also be considered improper.

Most urban residents, pastoralists, and farmers in the North speak a unique form of Arabic that has developed in Sudan. It is mutually intelligible to some extent with Egyptian Arabic but has some differences. This Sudanese Arabic is the language of trade.

Chadian Arabic is a regional variant of the language, found in the western part of the country and neighboring Chad. Two other variants, Najdi and Hejazi, are used in some northern and eastern areas.

The different forms of Arabic used in Sudan are only partly mutually intelligible, in the same way that Spanish and Portuguese speakers can understand a little of what a speaker of the other language is saying.

Like most other things in Sudan, language has become a political issue. As part of the government drive to Islamicize Sudan, great emphasis has been placed on the acquisition of Arabic. Most speakers of Arabic as a mother tongue are Muslim. Although some Muslims such as Nubians speak their own mother tongue, they also use Arabic, and the indigenous languages are expected to decline. In fact, eight indigenous languages are already extinct.

In the South and in the Nuba Mountains, refusing to speak Arabic is a means of resistance. The Nuba, who have been under intense pressure to abandon their culture, have chosen to teach their own languages in their schools. The Nuba and many organizations such as Amnesty International

A written language has existed in ancient Sudan since the third millennium BCE. Egyptian rulers left inscriptions on their tombs in Sudan written in Egyptian hieroglyphics. The African civilization that created the city of Meroë had its own written script, which was stylistically but not etymologically related to ancient Egyptian. The Meroitic script was first recorded in writing in the second century BCE. The script has two forms, hieroglyphic and cursive. The Meroitic hieroglyphic signs were borrowed from the Egyptians, while the cursive script is derived mainly from the Egyptian demotic script.

Many of the African languages had no written form of any kind before missionaries lived with the tribes who spoke them. Missionaries often became linguists not because of an interest in language for its own sake but because they wanted to bring the Bible to the African people, and the most efficient way to do that was to translate it into the local languages. So they learned the African languages, some learning tens of languages. They then created written forms by transcribing them into the Roman alphabet.

Even today, missionary societies keep vast databases of African languages, detailing where they are spoken, how many people speak them, and if they can be understood by other ethnic groups.

believe that the tribe's very existence is under threat, and speaking Nuba languages is one way of ensuring the tribe's survival until better times.

Arabic script, written from right to left, is based on a different system from that of the Roman alphabet. The Roman alphabet is not able to describe all the sounds in Arabic. Although written Arabic is somewhat similar to written Sudanese Arabic, some Arabic script cannot represent the actual words used by Sudanese Arabic speakers.

AFRICAN LANGUAGES

There are about one hundred African languages spoken in Sudan. They can be classified into groups based on certain similarities in grammar and structure, but they are mostly mutually incomprehensible. This gives us some indication of just how ancient African society is. The more unlike two languages from the same language family are, the longer the two must have been spoken in order for such differences to have evolved.

The thousand or so languages of Africa are divided into four major groups: Afro-Asiatic, Niger-Kordofanian, Nilo-Saharan, and Niger-Congo. Arabic belongs to the Hamito-Semitic branch of the Afro-Asiatic language family. Some of the languages spoken along the Red Sea coast of Sudan, including Bedawiya and Hausa, are also members of this language family. Hausa, a West African tongue, is spoken by about 489,000 people.

Most of the other African languages spoken in Sudan belong to a completely different group, the Nilo-Saharan family. Dinka, several Nuba languages, and Shilluk belong to this group. Some of these languages are mutually intelligible. For example, the language of the Fur people around Darfur is spoken by about one million people but can also be understood by speakers of Nyala, Laguri, and other languages spoken in the area.

Dinka is spoken in the South as a mother tongue and a lingua franca. It is also one of the major languages of South Sudan. It has wide regional differences but can be understood by the Nuer, who have their own language and live more or less exclusively in South Sudan.

LITERACY

Sudan has traditionally had poor literacy levels. With its hundreds of mother tongues, Sudan has had many problems in improving the rate of literacy. The government's plan to use Arabic as a unifying language of instruction in the 1970s only made matters worse. Not only were the people illiterate in their mother tongues, but they were illiterate in Arabic, too. Also, the years of civil war in Sudan did not help the literacy problem. Constant fighting and terrorizing from militants caused many schools to close. On top of that, there are many internally displaced Sudanese who are continually on the move, which makes education even more difficult. English and Arabic are both taught in schools now, as the official languages of the country. Sudan also has to overcome the mind-set that girls should be trained in domestic work and not educated.

Today 83 percent of men and 68.6 percent of women are able to read. This is a significant improvement upon a few decades ago, when the literacy rates for men and women were 45 percent and 18 percent respectively.

SUDANESE MEDIA

Before all privately owned newspapers were nationalized in 1970, Sudan had a large number of local and national newspapers. Political parties published a wealth of periodicals, and in Khartoum alone twenty-two daily papers were published—nineteen papers in Arabic and three in English. In all, Sudan had fifty-five daily or weekly newspapers and magazines. The media have since had a difficult time in Sudan, as each successive coup changed the direction of government. There are a few privately owned publications allowed today, and the government has bought controlling interests in 90 percent of the country's independent newspapers, ensuring that they do not take an anti-government stance. All publications are subjected to government censorship. In 2013, the government's National Intelligence and Security Service bought *Al-Sahafa* and *Al-Khartoum*, the nation's two leading independent newspapers. Publications that refused to sell were subject to heavy taxation, such as that imposed on *Al-Sudani* from 2006 to 2011, until they agreed to be bought out. Others have seen random seizures of their stock. For example, in May 2016 the government seized an entire print run of *Al-Ayam*, giving no reason for doing so. Most daily newspapers are in Arabic. A few English-

Literacy rates have improved greatly over the last few decades.

A newspaper stand in Khartoum

language newspapers exist, such as *Sudan Vision* and *Sudan Tribune.* These, too, are subject to heavy censorship and sometimes see themselves banned for extended periods of time.

As many as 80 percent of Sudanese in towns own a radio, but the percentage drops in the rural areas. Even so, many people have access to a radio for at least part of the day. Radio is therefore a more common medium for getting updates on news than television or newspapers. The Sudan National Radio Corporation is state owned and airs programming in Arabic, English, and some southern Sudan languages, offering a mixture of news, music, and cultural programs. People can also tune in to the Voice of America, Paris-based Radio Monte Carlo, and the BBC World Service. For a while, opposition radio stations such as the Voice of Sudan from the National Democratic Alliance and the Voice of Freedom and Renewal from the Sudan

Alliance Forces could be heard broadcasting via shortwave in Arabic and English, although such broadcasts have now become very rare, as a result of heavy government censorship.

Television is a rare luxury owned by the wealthy few and by some of the richer social clubs. Satellite dishes are a common sight in affluent areas. The one television station, Sudan National Broadcasting Corporation (SNBC), is government owned. There are no privately owned television stations bar a cable service jointly owned by the government and private investors. SNBC has a permanent military censor to ensure that news aired reflects official views. SNBC broadcasts sixty hours of programming a week, and a typical night's viewing consists of news broadcasts, farming information, religious programs, commercials, and lastly entertainment, which makes up about half of the broadcasting time.

INTERNET LINKS

http://arabicquick.com/an-introduction-to-the-arabic-language
This site provides a beginner's guide to Arabic.

http://www.sudantribune.com
This is the official website for one of Sudan's English-language newspapers.

https://sudan.usembassy.gov/sudanese_cultural_customs.html
This useful guide from the US Embassy in Sudan explains local greetings and customs.

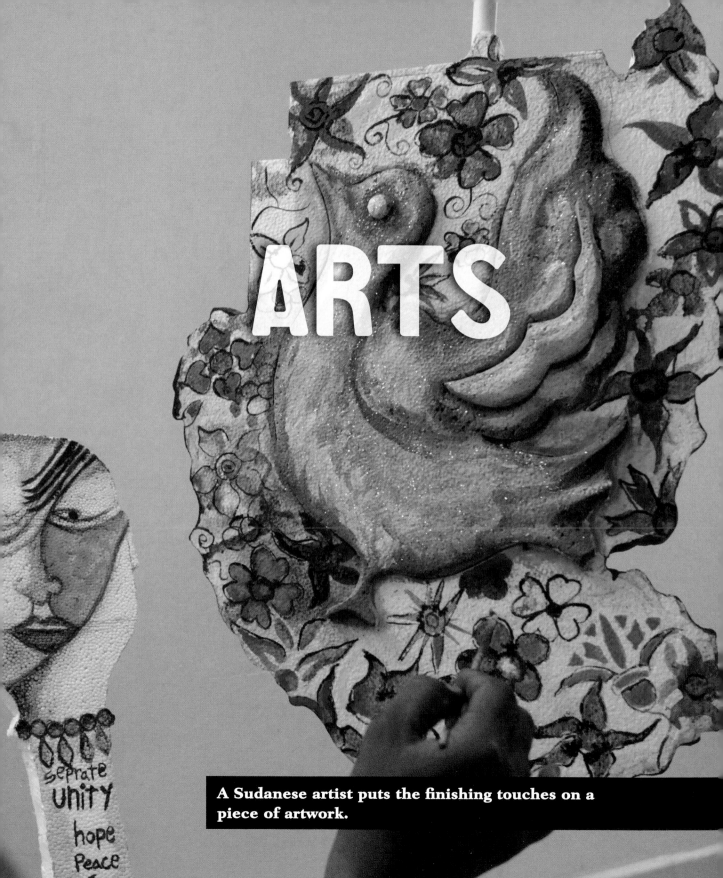

ARTS

A Sudanese artist puts the finishing touches on a piece of artwork.

10

"If you can walk, you can dance; if you can talk, you can sing."
—Sudanese proverb

SUDAN'S LONG, RICH HISTORY means it also has a long legacy of architecture and artwork. While ancient Egypt is known worldwide for its contributions to the development of civilization, Sudan's many kingdoms and cultures are lesser known. The remains of intricate monuments, temples, and palaces that still stand in Kerma and Meroë point to rich empires that acted as cultural meeting places for the Mediterranean, Africa, and Arabia. They represent the spots where this coming together of cultures resulted in a magnificence of art. In fact, Meroë is recognized as a UNESCO World Heritage Site because of its well-preserved pyramids and buildings from a long-bygone era.

Today, despite decades of war, famine, and struggle, Sudan continues to produce excellent musicians and artists who continue the nation's African and Arabic cultural traditions. The arts to be found in

LIBRARIES AND MUSEUMS

Sudan has about ten major libraries; two of the larger libraries are at the University of Khartoum and the Ahfad University for Women, with an estimated eight hundred thousand books. Other libraries include the Institute of Education, with about twenty-eight thousand volumes, and the Khartoum Polytechnic, with a collection of thirty thousand books. Minor libraries are maintained by secondary schools, places of worship, government agencies, and foreign community centers.

The National Museum in Khartoum

There are six museums, most of them in Khartoum. The National Museum, in the center of the city, has two floors depicting the ancient history of Sudan, with displays of the remains of the ancient Kush civilization and rescued frescoes from the early churches. In the garden of the museum are reconstructed temples of Buhen and Semna, salvaged during the construction of the Aswan Dam. The Temple of Buhen dates back to 1490 BCE and was built by the Egyptian queen Hatshepsut. Another ethnographic museum in Khartoum, which has since closed, was dedicated to artifacts of village life, many of which are still in use in parts of the country.

the country range from the traditional crafts of individual tribes—basket weaving, leatherwork, and such—to fine arts produced by students at the colleges in Khartoum. Likewise, music ranges from the traditional to the modern, and even hip-hop influences from the Western world can be heard.

ANCIENT MONUMENTS

One of the earlier sites of ancient architecture is Meroë, on the east bank of the Nile north of Khartoum. Meroë has many structures with Egyptian and Greco-Roman architectural influences, including the luxurious Royal City, dating back to the fourth century BCE, which is built inside an area of about 0.4 square miles (1 sq km). It is a walled city, within which is another walled area, believed to be the palace. The buildings, which are of sandstone and mud brick and are often faced with fired and glazed bricks, included audience chambers, shops, and temples. Most interesting, though, was an ornately decorated pool with a complex set of channels bringing water into it from a nearby well. About 3 miles (5 km) to the east stand the royal pyramids, where the past kings of Meroë are buried.

These statues of Nubian kings were excavated in Kerma.

Iron objects and pottery of a high quality have been found at many sites. The pottery was thrown on a potter's wheel, decorated, and fired. Many of the items are considered among the finest pottery objects found in Africa. Remains of textiles prove that cotton was grown and made into cloth here at a very early stage. There are still thousands of sites yet to be fully excavated in Sudan. The most recent significant find was by a group of archaeologists from the University of Geneva in Switzerland. In Kerma, south of the Third Cataract of the Nile, a pit was found filled with large monuments and finely carved statues of seven Nubian kings. These granite statues, 4 to 10 feet (1.2—3.1 m) tall, are highly polished, finely carved, and engraved with the name of the king on the back and feet of each sculpture. Smaller, more easily moved archaeological finds have been moved to several museums throughout Sudan.

COPTIC ART AND ARCHITECTURE

Coptic Christian culture dominated the Middle Nile from about the sixth century CE to the eighth century CE. Northern Sudan had several major

A preserved painting from an early Christian monastery in Faras

cities where the commercial, political, and social life was highly complex and structured. Many churches were in good condition when they were abandoned, and over the centuries they have filled with windblown sand. The remains of three cathedrals and at least one hundred churches dating from the fourth century to the fifteenth century have been found. The earlier buildings are bigger and grander than the later ones, suggesting that Christianity declined during this period.

Huge stones supported church columns and brick-lined vaults. Old Dongola was the capital of the kingdom of Makuria until the 1300s, and was home to many churches. The site was excavated in the 1960s by a team of Polish archaeologists. Today, only sandstone walls and columns remain. However, some of the frescoes and artifacts that were found are now on display at the National Museum in Khartoum. Another important early Christian archaeological site was at Faras, once part of the kingdom of Nobadia. This too was excavated in the 1960s, prior to being flooded for the construction of the Aswan Dam. The wall paintings were rescued before flooding and are on display in the National Museum in Warsaw, Poland.

In some sites, gold and glass lamps have been discovered, along with gold and silver jewelry set with precious stones. Further evidence indicates that gold and architectural stone were mined or excavated in Sudan and either used in the country or traded abroad.

ARCHITECTURE OF MODERN SUDAN

Just as in ancient times, architecture today says much about the spiritual and aesthetic life of a country. Modern Sudan's architectural masterpieces are its cathedrals and mosques. In Khartoum, the most interesting mosque is the Two Niles Mosque, which stands at the confluence of the Blue Nile and the White Nile. Opened in 1984, it is a huge dome-shape geometrical building, standing out stark and white against the browns and reds of the desert. Conical patterns around its base remind the observer of the many memorials to holy men that are scattered throughout the country. Another Khartoum mosque, built by King Farouk of Egypt, reflects a very different, almost colonial style of architecture. Its minaret and walls are ornately carved stone, more in keeping with the architecture of colonial Khartoum.

At El Obeid is a large Catholic cathedral in which many aspects of African culture come together. Smaller churches throughout Sudan are much simpler in design, in keeping with African architecture. They are simple wooden

Beautiful paintings adorn the walls of El Obeid Cathedral.

or mud-walled buildings with straw roofs, which like most other African architecture will eventually disappear, leaving no evidence of their existence.

TRADITIONAL CRAFTS

Craftwork is still an important element in daily Sudanese life. In the West, crafts have become an expensive rarity, but in Sudan, everyday objects are handmade using ancient techniques. Domestic objects are woven using palm leaves or grasses, and complex woodcarving is still in evidence. The goods carved range from small, simple household items to large, elaborately decorated tables and beds. In Port Sudan, now quite run down since Sudanese exports have declined, the older buildings still display elegant latticework in their window frames and doorways. In nearby Suakin, the crumbling buildings show elegant architecture made from coral stone, which is gradually being eroded by the desert winds.

A potter makes his wares.

Crafts workers producing objects in gold, silver, and brass can be found in any souk in Sudan. Some ethnic groups wear exquisite silver and gold jewelry or carry ornate decorative swords, daggers, and knives, all of which one can see being made in the marketplace. Elaborate leather goods are made by the nomadic tribes to barter for food. The Baggara women are particularly famous for their elaborately patterned leather blankets adorned with cowrie shells. Many of the southern tribes wear ornate necklaces made from ivory and precious stones. For the small tourist industry, there are many carvings in ebony and other precious woods.

STORYTELLING

Sudan has an ancient tradition of storytelling. Some stories told around firesides in Sudan have existed in one form or another for centuries. Many of the languages of Sudan had no written form until the missionaries began to transcribe them, so history and legends were handed down from one generation to another in an oral tradition.

In modern times, men and women have found a voice in Sudanese society by retelling some of the ancient tales and creating new ones to record the lifestyles of the Sudanese. One modern Sudanese writer is Tayeb Salih, who wrote fictionalized accounts of the life of Sudanese people. His books include *The Wedding of Zein* and his best-known work, *The Season of Migration to the North*, both of which were published in English translation in 1969. Other writers include the controversially outspoken feminist Kola Boof, Leila Aboulela, Hammour Ziada, and Mansour El Souwaim.

Sudanese author
Tayeb Salih

TRADITIONAL MUSIC

The people of Africa have used percussion and string instruments as part of their religious worship and daily life for centuries, and the Sudanese are no exception. Many types of instruments, such as the drum known as the tambour among the Nubians and the *rababa* (RA-bah-bah), a stringed instrument, can be heard at religious celebrations and tribal dances.

The Dinka record all their activities, especially wars, initiations, and other major life events, in song. Through their songs, the people can reinforce their identity, recall their ancestors, praise their group, or settle a dispute. Because they enshrine the history, beliefs, and values of the Dinka, many of their songs are about their all-important cattle.

SUDANESE MUSICIANS

Abdel Gadir Salim, Abdel Aziz el Mubarak, and Mohamed Gubara are popular Sudanese musicians whose music has been brought to the West through albums and performances.

Salim fronts a small ensemble of oud, tabla (a kind of drum), and accordion, highlighting the rhythms and melodies as well as the voice of the artist. He also plays with a larger band.

Mubarak sings with oud, drum, and accordion. His influences are broader than Salim's, with traces of many other cultures slipping into his more urban interpretation. Gubara plays with a tambour. His sharper vocal style and sparse accompaniment create stunning music with an almost chilling intensity and energy.

Other contemporary Sudanese musicians include Wafir, who is considered a virtuoso on the accordion, the violin, and the oud, and Hassouna Bangladish, who plays traditional Sudanese music with a contemporary feel.

The popular music of the North is influenced by the sounds, language, and instruments of Arabic culture. Khartoum and Omdurman have recording facilities that are accessible to rising talents as well as to established masters, and the wealth of popular music is disseminated through radio and inexpensive cassettes.

MODERN MUSIC

Western influences have made themselves felt in more recent years as hip-hop has grown in popularity in Sudan. Hip-hop has been used around the world by youth who feel that they are ignored by mainstream society and politicians. Through their music, they can reach out to others who feel the same, sharing a voice of unity and finding an outlet to express frustrations about, in Sudan's case, such topics as ongoing violence and a desire for peace. The songs may also be a way of reaching those who might otherwise have no way of hearing alternative political messages. For example, some hip-hop stars use songs about an end to violence and the importance of education as a means of teaching child soldiers that there is a different way forward. Popular Sudanese hip-hop artists are Bangs, who moved to Australia as a teen, and Bas, raised in America since the age of eight.

Although frowned upon by Islamic society, hip-hop has become very popular among young Sudanese.

Hip-hop music is widely seen as a form of political defiance in Sudan, and while people sing about peace, several artists have been badly beaten by local police while performing in their home country.

INTERNET LINKS

http://www.sudanembassy.org/index.php/modern-and-contemporay-art
Information about modern and contemporary art comes from the Sudanese Embassy.

http://whc.unesco.org/en/list/1336
This UNESCO website discusses the treasures of Meroë.

LEISURE

A man drives his camels across the desert to market.

SUDAN HAS LONG SUFFERED FROM ongoing civil war, famine, and social unrest, and so it may seem strange to think of anyone having the time or opportunity for leisure activities. However, those living in Khartoum and other larger cities remain rather sheltered from the problems that plague the western part of the country. For them, life continues in a manner similar to what we might recognize—work, family, and relaxation.

Given the climate, many workplaces are open in the morning and later afternoon/early evening, with an extended break during the hottest part of the day. Work typically finishes at about 8 p.m. Afterwards, men often go to a club to relax, eat, socialize with friends, and perhaps participate in some form of sporting or leisure activity. Women have less freedom to socialize in public. They stay at home, caring for the children and their elderly relatives. Preparing meals and keeping the house tidy takes up much of their time.

RELAXATION

Most towns are empty, dark places after sundown. However, there are an increasing number of restaurants, a number of movie theaters, and

11

A very popular sport in Sudan is soccer (which they call football). There is a national league, and some towns have two or more teams in the Sudan Premier League.

Khartoum's Afra Mall features all the conveniences of modern city life.

more street lighting. Many of the nightlife activities common in the West, however, are disapproved of. This was not the case before the declaration of sharia law. Khartoum had a reputation as a "fast" town with all kinds of nightlife and bars that sold local and imported alcohol.

In the long, hot afternoons, for those who do not sleep, there are many tea shops to visit to hear the latest gossip or to read the daily paper. In many societies, shopping has become a leisure activity. To some extent, this is true in Sudan. People go to shopping malls and the souk, which is liveliest in the early morning and where mostly men or older women go to do each day's shopping. In some towns there are newly arrived nomadic groups from Darfur and Kordofan with gossip from their last port of call or new shipments of scarce goods to look over. People can be seen meeting up at the Camel Market, west of Khartoum.

POPULAR SPORTS

The market is an important center of social life in Sudan.

A very popular sport in Sudan is soccer (which they call football). There is a national league, and some towns have two or more teams in the Sudan Premier League. The major sporting clubs in Khartoum are al-Hilal, Mareikh, and Morada. Al-Hilal often tops the football league. Where there is a television, European matches are watched avidly. Even the most remote communities in Sudan are likely to have a soccer team. In 1970, Sudan's national team won the African Cup of Nations, although they have not been able to repeat that success since then.

Wrestling is a famous tradition among the Nuba. This activity contributed to the Nuba's problems when they became a major tourist attraction in the 1970s and early 1980s. The Muslim government decided that the naked

Nuba wrestling

wrestling and dancing was irreligious, and the campaign to clothe and "civilize" the Nuba began. It is still possible to see Nuba wrestling on most Fridays in the Haj Yusef district of Khartoum North. The sport is different from Western-style wrestling in that there is no pinning. Instead, it takes the form of standing grappling.

Sudan has always been a country where fine horses were bred, and Khartoum has a racecourse that is patronized by many of its citizens. Races are held on Fridays and Sundays, and polo matches are held on Wednesdays and Saturdays. Gambling on the races is illegal, but some bets continue under the table.

Other than their passion for football, most Sudanese have little time or money for sports. Some sports are organized in expatriate settlements that spring up as groups of aid workers arrive. Some settlements have a swimming pool; others have table tennis and other activities to keep the workers occupied. The expatriate community is biggest in Khartoum and is organized around national clubs.

CHILDREN AT PLAY

Children in the West have a lot of leisure time, but for many children in Sudan, games have to take second place to survival. Most rural children work alongside their mothers in the fields if they are not in school, and many spend a large part of each day traveling to and from the nearest source of water. Children as young as five are left in charge of their younger brothers and sisters. Some nomadic children spend their days in charge of their animals. When children do have leisure time, it is spent perhaps in finding a use for pieces of scrap metal, bending them into the shapes of toys to sell to other people, or making kites from sticks and old plastic welded together with a burning cigarette.

TELLING STORIES

One traditional activity that survives in Sudan is storytelling. Stories are passed on from older generations to the young. The Sudanese of the South share many of the folk stories of other areas of Africa, such as the stories of Anansi the spider—a story that also came to America with the Africans taken into slavery in the eighteenth and nineteenth centuries.

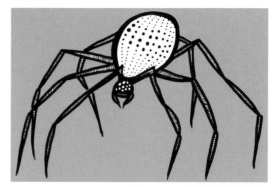

Other stories concern ghosts or history. One modern story tells of a tree outside an old prison in Kassala that was used to hang criminals. Local people believed that the suffering spirits of those executed lived in the tree. The tree died and was cut down to be used for firewood, but no one in the village would touch it. When a passing traveler took some of the wood and lit a fire, he heard the voices of the dead people calling out to him from the flames.

INTERNET LINKS

http://anansistories.com
This website is devoted to the traditional Anansi stories and folklore.

http://www.fifa.com/associations/association=sdn/index.html
Here you can read FIFA news and updates about Sudan's favorite sport.

http://ngm.nationalgeographic.com/ngm/0302/feature3/index.html?fs=www3.nationalgeographic.com&fs=plasma.nationalgeographic.com
This National Geographic article explores the Nuba and their love of wrestling.

FESTIVALS

Muslims gather for prayer to mark the end of Ramadan.

FESTIVALS AND HOLIDAYS REMAIN an important part of Sudanese culture and are a way to forget about hardships for a while. The major public holidays are Independence Day, on January 1, and Revolution Day, on June 30. Revolution Day celebrates the 1989 National Islamic Front military coup over the previous democratically elected government. Most other major holidays are to mark festivals of the Muslim calendar. Coptic Christmas is celebrated in early January.

12

Maulid an-Nabi (the birthday of the Prophet Muhammad) is a holiday especially enjoyed by children. They eat pink sugar dolls and sticky sweets.

ISLAMIC CELEBRATIONS

There are two major religious festivals for Sudanese Muslims: Eid al-Fitr (EED AHL-fitr), which marks the end of Ramadan, and Eid al-Adha (EED AHL-ad-ah), which commemorates Abraham's being asked to sacrifice his son. Another day that many children look forward to is the Prophet Muhammad's birthday, Maulid an-Nabi (MAU-lid an-nah-bee). Other Islamic celebrations include Laylat al-Qadar (LEE-lat AHL-ka-dar), celebrating the night of the first revelation of the Quranic verses to Muhammad; Israwal Miraj (is-RAH wal ME-raj),

Markets are filled with sweets for religious festivals.

commemorating the Prophet's night journey from Mecca to Jerusalem and his ascension to establish the five pillars of the Islamic faith; and Muharram (moo-HAR-rahm), commemorating the martyrdom of the Prophet Muhammad's grandson, Hussein, who was killed in battle.

Muslim festivals are all based upon the Islamic calendar, and so are based upon the moon's rotation. There are still twelve months, of either twenty-nine or thirty days, but the lunar year is ten or eleven days shorter than the Gregorian solar year, which is the basis of the Western calendar. As a result, Muslim festivals are not held on the same date of the Gregorian calendar each year; it takes thirty-three years for a complete lunar-calendar cycle.

EID AL-FITR During Ramadan, the month of fasting, the breaking of the fast each day occurs at the moment of dusk. Each evening becomes a feast as the family settles down to enjoy the success of another day's fasting. Eid al-Fitr, which begins on the first day of the tenth month, marks the end of Ramadan. Not surprisingly, it is characterized by feasting during the day. From a religious point of view, Eid al-Fitr signifies the glorious culmination of a period of spiritual cleansing and purification.

Eid al-Fitr is the most festive period of the year for Sudanese Muslims. It is celebrated with large family meals that all members of an extended family will try to attend. Toward the end of Ramadan, the family home will be thoroughly cleaned in preparation. If there is money for new clothes or new furniture, this is the time when the shopping will be done. During the four days of celebration, people wear their new clothes and visit friends and relatives. Eid al-Fitr is a cross between Thanksgiving and Christmas, being a religious, family, and social festival. Children receive gifts at this time of the year.

EID AL-ADHA   This festival commemorates Abraham's willingness to sacrifice his son for God. It is also celebrated to mark the end of the hajj pilgrimage to Mecca. Muslims who can afford it sacrifice a sheep on the feast day and give a portion of the meat to the poor.

A huge feast is prepared for Eid al-Fitr.

THE CEREMONIES OF NORTHERN SUDAN

Two interesting ceremonies are practiced in northern Sudan. The *zar* ceremony is an opportunity for women to engage in activity outside the house, while the *zikr* ceremony is a religious ceremony for men.

Many women spend long periods of their life in the home, so festivals are often an occasion for women to go out and mix more freely than usual. The zar ceremony is held to help women who may be emotionally troubled. The ceremony is thought to soothe the spirits that possess them. The highlight of the ceremony is a dance where women beat out a rhythm with drums and rattles, and troubled women get to their feet to dance to the music. A woman might have a particular object or talisman associated with the spirit that troubles her, and she will dance holding this object. The ceremony sometimes lasts as long as seven days.

Meanwhile, the Muslim zikr ceremony is regularly performed in the bigger towns of northern Sudan. The men who take part in the ceremony are known as whirling dervishes. They believe that through the rhythm and movement of dance they can gain a personal state of rapture and so commune with God. The men, wearing long white jallabiya and turbans, meet near a holy place, which is usually the grave of a holy person. The holy men who conduct the ceremony wear traditional colorful patched clothes.

Men move to the rhythm of drums, and from time to time one will break away from the crowd and whirl himself into a state of religious ecstasy.

Women dance the *zar* ceremony to expel demons.

Young boys practice the dance at the outskirts of the crowd, and the occasional woman may join in, much to the disapproval of the men. The ceremony takes place on Friday evenings as dusk approaches and continues until night has fallen. In Omdurman, this ceremony has become a tourist attraction.

CHRISTMAS

Christian festivals are still an important part of daily life for some in Sudan. Catholics celebrate the coming of Christmas with midnight Mass. Many families spend the day together. Christians give gifts and eat a special Christmas lunch—a Sudanese feast rather than the traditional Western lunch.

Instead of the traditional December 25 Christmas, some celebrate Coptic Christmas on January 7. Since the South Sudan split, the number of Christians in Sudan has decreased. The government reports that 3 percent of the population are Christian, but some in Khartoum say the number is actually as high as 15 percent. They believe that the government may be reporting incorrect numbers to help with the imposition of sharia law.

ANIMIST FESTIVALS

Since the independence of South Sudan, there are fewer people in the country who still practice animist religions. However, there are still small rural pockets in the South where remaining Shilluk and Dinka populations can be found.

Animist festivals are usually associated with the cycles of nature, such as harvests, changes of the seasons, the rise and fall of the Nile, and the coming of rain. The Shilluk have two major festivals, the rain dance and the harvest festival. Both festivals involve dance and offerings to the ancestors. They and the Dinka also have fishing festivals where hundreds of men go into the river in the Sudd to catch as many fish as possible.

Many animist tribes practice animal sacrifice. To celebrate a special day (or to ward off danger or illness), the Dinka and Nuer tribes will sacrifice one of their cattle. They believe that performing the ritual brings a benevolent spiritual presence to the occasion. The ritual sacrifice involves long speeches and many gestures with the spear, and when the animal is slaughtered it is shared among the whole community according to strict laws of division. The ritual itself, rather than the death of the animal, is most important; if the Nuer have no ox available, they will substitute a nonedible cucumber and perform the rites in exactly the same way, even calling the cucumber "ox."

Dinka celebrate the cattle festival.

INTERNET LINKS

http://www.iexplore.com/articles/travel-guides/africa/sudan/festivals-and-events
Here you can explore some of the key festivals in the country.

http://www.touregypt.net/featurestories/zar.htm
This illustrated article discusses the zar ceremony.

http://www.webexhibits.org/calendars/calendar-islamic.html
This is a helpful explanation of the Islamic calendar and how it correlates to the Western (Gregorian) calendar.

FOOD

Ful, a bean dish, is a common dish in Sudan.

13

FAMINE AND WIDESPREAD POVERTY in parts of Sudan mean food is a precious commodity. Nevertheless, nomadic peoples have, for centuries, relied on the hospitality of communities as they have traveled, and they have reciprocated when welcoming guests. Modern visitors to Sudan note the warm welcome they receive from the Sudanese people and can share many a story about being invited to share a meal with newly made friends.

Grains are staples of the Sudanese diet, particularly rice, sorghum, and millet. Unleavened flatbreads are popular. One such bread, called *kisra* (KISS-rah), is made from sorghum. Another important dish is *ful* (FOOL), made of beans. It is often served with raw onions. Other foods are based upon regional availability. For example, lentils and vegetables can be grown in the fertile lands of the Nile Valley.

FRESH FOOD

In the desert regions, vegetables and fresh fruit are a rare luxury. Ful and kisra may be the only things people eat for weeks on end. In the South, where it rains regularly, there are citrus fruits and many varieties of vegetables to make a varied and interesting diet.

"Better a meal of vegetables where there is love than a fatted ox where there is hatred."
—Sudanese proverb

Meat consumption is common all over Sudan. However, because of the high cost and short storage life of meat, Sudanese find ways to extend the meat's shelf life. One way the Sudanese preserve meat is to dry it, cut it into strips, and then add the strips to stews. Favorite meats are lamb and chicken. Many people eat fish caught from the Nile or the lakes in the mountains. Fish is often eaten for breakfast.

There is very little processed food or refrigeration in rural areas, so most food is bought fresh daily from the souk. Some fruits and food are only seasonally available.

ILLEGAL ALCOHOL

Under sharia law, alcohol is forbidden to all citizens of Sudan, but illegal brews are made

Fruit sellers

in remote areas and enjoyed by many people. *Aragi* (ah-rah-gi) is distilled from dates and is a little like white rum. In other areas, *tedj* (TAY-dj), a wine made from fermented honey, is preferred. A beer called *merissa* (mer-EE-sah) is brewed from sorghum and dates. It is easily available in the South.

DAILY MEALS

Most Sudanese start their day with a cup of very sweet milky tea called *shai bi laban* (SHY bee LA-bahn). Throughout the cities and small towns and at intervals along all routes there are women with simple tea-making equipment ready to serve this breakfast staple.

The first meal of the day comes after the first of the morning's work, at around 9:30. For the better-off, this is often a dish with liver, such as cooked liver with ful and fish, or raw lungs and liver served with hot chili. *Kibda* (KEEB-da), a dish of fried chopped liver, is a popular breakfast food.

A second meal is eaten in the evening and might be vegetable stew with ful, salad, and if the family can afford it, a piece of mutton or beef. In the evening, a drink of hot sweetened milk called *laban* (LA-bahn) is popular. Often the milk is flavored with nutmeg.

A family gathers to share a meal.

THE FEAST

As the guests arrive, they are offered a cooling drink such as freshly squeezed citrus juice or *kerkadey* (KAYRK-ah-deh), made from the hibiscus flower and sweetened with sugar. The offering of drinks is a symbolic gesture welcoming the guests after their "long journey."

After freshening up, the guests are taken to the dining room, which is decorated with peacock feathers. Men and women are served in separate areas. At the center of the dining room is a low table surrounded by large, comfortable cushions. A pitcher containing water and a large bowl are brought in, and guests' hands are washed.

A jebena is the traditional pot used to prepare coffee.

The meal begins with soup brought out already served in bowls carried on a huge aluminum or brass tray. Each guest is given a bowl, which is held in the left hand while a spoon is held in the right. When the guests have finished, they return the bowl and the spoon to the tray, which is then taken away.

The next tray carries the five or six remaining dishes of the meal, including kisra, which is used to scoop up the sauces. The host serves each person a piece of bread and a bowl of salad, and guests help themselves to food from the other dishes. Chili is served in little individual bowls. Food is eaten with a spoon or the right hand.

For a very special occasion, an animal will be slaughtered. The menu might be *shorba*, a soup sometimes made from pureed lamb; *mashi*, tomatoes and eggplants stuffed with rice and minced lamb; *gammonia*, stewed sheep's stomach, served with tomatoes and onions; a salad of tomatoes, lettuce, onions, and green peppers with a lime-juice dressing; *shata*, a little bowl of hot chili to add to the dishes; kisra; fresh fruit segments; and coffee.

The hand-washing ritual is carried out again after the main course, and then dessert is served. There are very few cooked Sudanese desserts. Usually fresh fruit is peeled and served in segments, but there are a few more complicated dishes, such as a dessert very similar to crème caramel.

After the food, *jebena* coffee is served. This is named after the pot in which it is prepared. If guests prefer, they can have *qahwa bi habahan* (KAH-wa bee HA-ba-han), which is sweet hot coffee spiced with cardamom.

Food in Sudan varies from one ethnic group to another. Differences in lifestyles and climates account for the types of food favored by a particular region. Northern Sudan is known for its simple wheat-based cuisine. The staple dish, gourrassa (GOO-rahs-sa), is made of wheat flour and baked into a circular shape. In eastern Sudan, the Ethiopian-influenced banana-paste dish called moukhbaza (MOOK-bah-za) is very popular. In the nomadic West, milk and dairy products are commonplace and are used in most of the cooking. The western region is also known for its cereal called dukhun (DOO-koon), which is used as a base for preparing thick porridges and stews. Central Sudan has a popular fish dish cooked with onions, spices, and tomato sauce called fassikh (FAS-sikh). Because vegetables and fish are more abundant in the South, the region is well known for its fish stew called kajaik (KA-jay-eek), which is usually eaten with aseeda (AH-see-da), a porridge made of sorghum.

Finally the guests relax around the table while an incense burner filled with sandalwood is brought into the room to perfume the air.

DINING TABOOS

The Islamic rules regarding which foods are "clean" apply in Sudan, where the majority of people are Muslim. Pork is not eaten in Muslim households (except among the Nuba, who believe that it is acceptable to eat pork and also to drink alcohol). Muslim law also prohibits eating shellfish, but this is not commonly available in Sudan anyway. Muslims eat only with the right hand, believing that the left hand is unclean as it is used strictly for bathroom ablutions.

THE KITCHEN

Because Sudan is one of the hottest countries in the world, most traditional or rural cooking takes place outside the house. Cooking is done outside over an open fire, which is often set in a hollow in the ground, with low mud walls around the sides. Balanced on the mud walls is a huge wok-like metal pot in which thick vegetable and meat stews are boiled. The fire is fueled with kindling collected from the bush. Cooking utensils, spoons, cups, and plates are made from natural products, such as gourds, large leaves, or wood from the date palm.

In the countryside, there is little running water—water is stored in animal skins, in pottery jars, or in oil drums to which wheels have been added to make the trips to the well easier. In some places, the trunks of baobab trees are hollowed out and waterproofed with pitch to serve as water tanks.

Nomadic cooking facilities are quite similar except that they are small enough to be packed away and moved. In the desert, there is less firewood to be found, so cooking is done very carefully using animal dung as fuel. In many areas of Sudan, the ash from this type of fire is used as an effective mosquito repellent. Animal skins are used to store water and to make tents, and cooking

In rural areas, food is still prepared in a pot over the fire.

implements may be made of bone. Rather than growing all their own food, the nomads must visit towns to barter goods for fresh vegetables and enough sorghum and beans to last until their next visit to a town.

City kitchens are a little more sophisticated, but poorer people still cook outdoors over charcoal stoves. Many dishes such as meat kebabs and grilled liver are cooked directly over the coals, like a Western barbecue. There is piped water in some areas, although it is generally untreated water piped straight from the river. People have to boil their drinking water to kill the parasites that live in it. Plastic and metal kitchen utensils are bought from the souk.

Baobab trees, with their thick trunks, are useful as water tanks.

INTERNET LINKS

http://marktanner.com/sudan-recipes/index.html
This website provides a collection of traditional Sudanese recipes compiled by two former volunteers in the country.

http://www.sudanembassy.org/index.php/sudanese-food
The Sudan Embassy details key dishes on this website.

DAMA DE POTAATAS (SPICED POTATOES WITH BEEF)

6 onions

4 tablespoons tomato paste

⅓ cup oil

3 cloves of crushed garlic

½ pound beef steak

3 cups water

3 tomatoes

½ green pepper

1 teaspoon salt

1 teaspoon cardamom

1 teaspoon cinnamon

2 potatoes

Chop onions. Fry in a pot with the oil at medium heat. Keep covered, stirring occasionally. Add the water and cover. Cook for 5 to 10 minutes until the water is almost evaporated. Add the chopped tomatoes to the pot. Peel and chop the potatoes and fry them in a separate pan until golden. Chop the steak into small pieces and add to the pot with chopped green pepper, salt, cardamom, and cinnamon. Cover and cook for 3 minutes. Add tomato paste and stir, adding water until smooth and runny. Add potatoes, cover, and leave to simmer for 10 minutes, adding more water occasionally. Stir in crushed garlic before serving. This serves 4 people.

BASEEMA (SUDANESE LEMON CAKE)

5 eggs
1 cup powdered sugar
¾ cup butter
1 teaspoon vanilla extract
2 cups yogurt
2 teaspoons baking powder
2 cups flour
1 cup shredded coconut

Glaze:
1½ cups sugar
1 tablespoon lemon juice
1 cup water

In a bowl, beat the eggs together with the powdered sugar. Add the butter, vanilla extract, and yogurt, and mix well. In a separate bowl, sift the flour, baking powder, and coconut. Add to the egg mixture and stir until all the ingredients are combined. Pour into a greased baking tray and bake for 30 minutes at 400ºF (200ºC). Remove the cake from the oven and poke holes in it with a fork while it is cooling.

In a saucepan, mix the sugar, lemon juice, and water. Bring to a boil until it thickens into a syrup. Pour the syrup over the cake. Cut the cake into squares to serve.

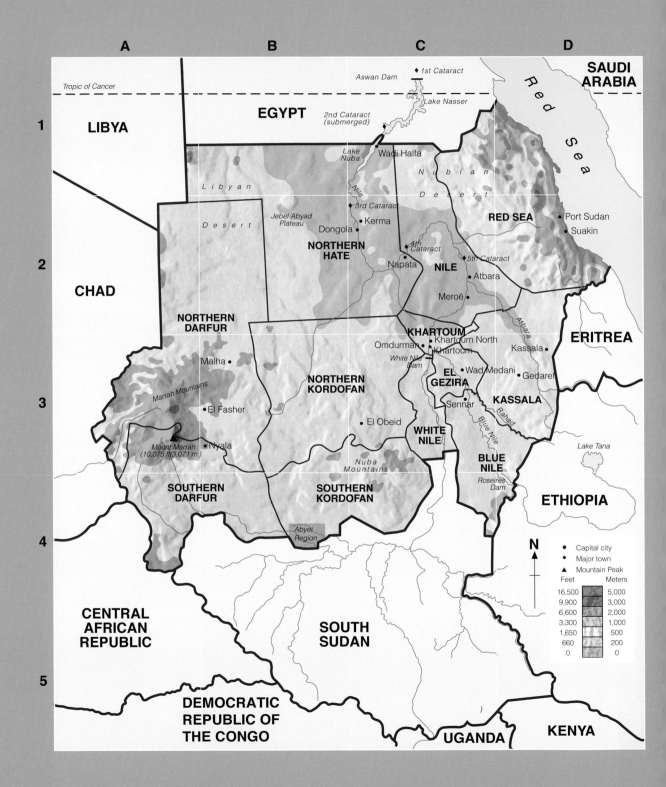

MAP OF SUDAN

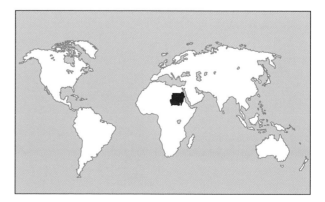

ECONOMIC SUDAN

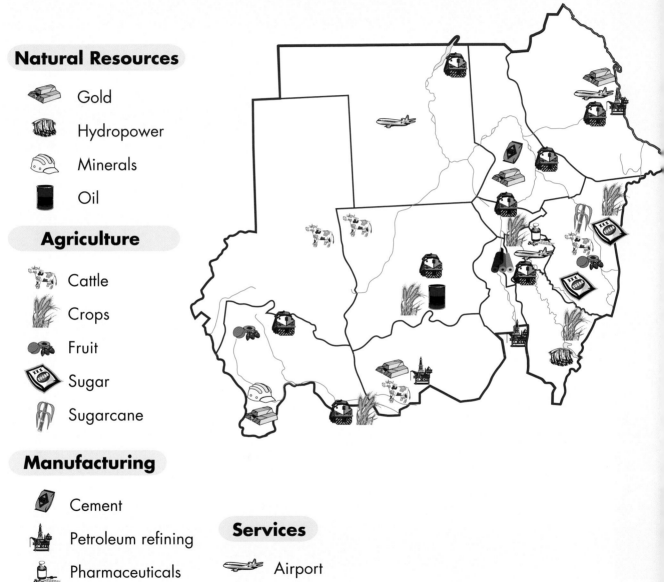

Natural Resources

- Gold
- Hydropower
- Minerals
- Oil

Agriculture

- Cattle
- Crops
- Fruit
- Sugar
- Sugarcane

Manufacturing

- Cement
- Petroleum refining
- Pharmaceuticals
- Textiles

Services

- Airport
- Railway

ABOUT THE ECONOMY

OVERVIEW

Ongoing social conflicts and civil war have caused many problems for Sudan's economy. This was worsened in 2011, when South Sudan seceded, and Sudan lost three-quarters of its oil production. Since then, Sudan has been struggling to rebuild its economic growth, striving to lower expenditure while developing other non-oil sources of revenue. Inflation reached a peak of 47 percent in 2012 but has since fallen to 18 percent.

GROSS DOMESTIC PRODUCT (GDP)

$81.44 billion (2015 estimate)

GDP GROWTH

4.9 percent (2015 estimate)

LAND USE

Agricultural: 100 percent, of which permanent pasture: 84.2 percent; arable land: 15.7 percent; permanent crops: 0.2 percent

CURRENCY

1 Sudanese pound (SDG) = 100 piastres
Notes: 50, 20, 10, 5, 2 pounds
Coins: 1 pound; 50, 20, 10, 5, 1 piastres
USD1 = SDG 6.35 (2016)

NATURAL RESOURCES

Petroleum; small reserves of iron ore, copper, chromium ore, zinc, tungsten, mica, silver, gold; hydropower

AGRICULTURAL PRODUCTS

Banana, cotton, groundnut, gum arabic, mango, millet, papaya, sesame, sorghum, sugarcane, sweet potato, tapioca, wheat

INDUSTRIES

Armaments, automobile assembly, cement, cotton ginning, edible oil, oil, petroleum refining, pharmaceuticals, sugar, soap distilling, shoes, textiles

MAJOR EXPORTS

Gold, oil and petroleum products, cotton, livestock, groundnut, gum arabic, sesame, sugar

MAJOR IMPORTS

Foodstuff, manufactured goods, medicine and chemicals, refinery and transport equipment, textiles, wheat

MAJOR TRADING PARTNERS

China, Saudi Arabia, United Arab Emirates, Egypt, Australia, Turkey, India (2015 estimates)

INFLATION RATE

18 percent (2015 estimate)

CULTURAL SUDAN

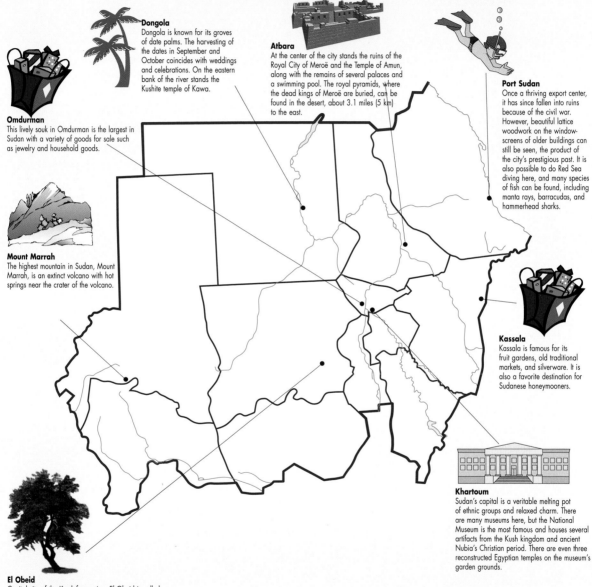

Dongola
Dongola is known for its groves of date palms. The harvesting of the dates in September and October coincides with weddings and celebrations. On the eastern bank of the river stands the Kushite temple of Kawa.

Atbara
At the center of the city stands the ruins of the Royal City of Meroë and the Temple of Amun, along with the remains of several palaces and a swimming pool. The royal pyramids, where the dead kings of Meroë are buried, can be found in the desert, about 3.1 miles (5 km) to the east.

Port Sudan
Once a thriving export center, it has since fallen into ruins because of the civil war. However, beautiful lattice woodwork on the window-screens of older buildings can still be seen, the product of the city's prestigious past. It is also possible to do Red Sea diving here, and many species of fish can be found, including manta rays, barracudas, and hammerhead sharks.

Omdurman
This lively souk in Omdurman is the largest in Sudan with a variety of goods for sale such as jewelry and household goods.

Mount Marrah
The highest mountain in Sudan, Mount Marrah, is an extinct volcano with hot springs near the crater of the volcano.

Kassala
Kassala is famous for its fruit gardens, old traditional markets, and silverware. It is also a favorite destination for Sudanese honeymooners.

Khartoum
Sudan's capital is a veritable melting pot of ethnic groups and relaxed charm. There are many museums here, but the National Museum is the most famous and houses several artifacts from the Kush kingdom and ancient Nubia's Christian period. There are even three reconstructed Egyptian temples on the museum's garden grounds.

El Obeid
Capital city of the Kordofan region, El Obeid is called "the gum arabic capital of the world." It was once the Mahdi's capital and political center. The Roman Catholic cathedral here is impressive with beautiful paintings of the Virgin and Child on its chancel.

ABOUT THE CULTURE

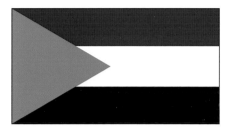

OFFICIAL NAME
Jumhuriyat as-Sudan (Republic of the Sudan)

FLAG DESCRIPTION
Three equal horizontal bands of red (on top), white, and black, with a green isosceles triangle on the hoist side

CAPITAL
Khartoum

POPULATION
36,700,000 (2016 estimate)

RELIGIOUS GROUPS
Sunni Muslim: 97 percent; indigenous beliefs: 1.5 percent; Christian: 1.5 percent

ETHNIC GROUPS
Sudanese Arab: 70 percent; remaining 30 percent a combination of Beja, Fur, Nuba, and Fallata

BIRTHRATE
28.5 births per 1,000 Sudanese (2016 estimate)

DEATH RATE
7.5 deaths per 1,000 Sudanese (2016 estimate)

LITERACY RATE
75.9 percent (2015 estimate)

MAIN LANGUAGES
Arabic (official), English (official), Nubian, Tu Bedawie, Fur

NATIONAL HOLIDAYS
Independence Day (January 1), Eid al-Adha (date varies), Islamic New Year (date varies), Prophet Muhammad's Birthday (date varies), Revolution Day (June 30), Eid al-Fitr (date varies)

LEADERS IN POLITICS
Ibrahim Abboud—first president of independent Sudan (1958—1964)
Jaafar al-Nimeiry—president of military government of Sudan (1969—1985)
Sayyid Sadiq al-Mahdi—current leader of Umma Party and prime minister of coalition government of Sudan (1966—1967 and 1986—1989)
Omar Hassan al-Bashir—president of Sudan (1989—present)
John Garang—late Dinka leader and founder/leader of SPLA (1983—2005) and first vice president of Sudan (July 2005)
Salva Kiir Mayardit—vice president of Sudan (2005—2011); president of South Sudan (2011—present)
Bakri Hassan Saleh—first vice president of Sudan (2013—present)
Hasabu Mohamed Abdel Rahmin—second vice president of Sudan (2013—present)

TIMELINE

IN SUDAN	IN THE WORLD
1504–1821 Funj kingdom, the largest of the Arab sultanates, controls central Sudan.	
	1530 Beginning of transatlantic slave trade organized by the Portuguese in Africa.
1821 Egypt conquers the Funj kingdom.	
	1861 The US Civil War begins.
1877 The British and the Turks establish their authority in the region.	
1881–1885 Muhammad Ahmad, the Mahdi, leads a revolt against Egypt and captures Khartoum.	
1885–1898 Reign of the Mahdi and Khalifa Abdullahi.	
1898–1899 British and Egyptian forces invade Sudan and begin Anglo-Egyptian rule.	
	1914–1918 World War I begins.
	1939–1945 World War II begins.
1956 Sudan becomes an independent republic.	
	1957 The Russians launch *Sputnik 1.*
1958 First military coup against the civilian government. General Ibrahim Abboud becomes president.	
1964 The October Revolution.	
	1966–1969 The Chinese Cultural Revolution.
1969 A second military coup brings Colonel Jaafar al-Nimeiry to power. He is "elected" president.	
1972 Al-Nimeiry signs a peace agreement giving the South autonomous regional government.	
1985 Al-Nimeiry is overthrown by a military coup.	
1986 A coalition government is formed, with Sayyid Sadiq al-Mahdi elected as prime minister.	**1986** Nuclear power disaster at Chernobyl in Ukraine.

IN SUDAN	IN THE WORLD
1989 Brigadier General Omar Hassan al-Bashir overthrows the al-Mahdi government.	
	1991 Breakup of the Soviet Union.
1996 The South boycotts the general elections, and al-Bashir is "elected" president.	
	1997 Hong Kong is returned to China.
2000 Al-Bashir is "reelected."	
2001 Peace talks between al-Bashir and John Garang fail.	**2001** Terrorists crash planes in New York, Washington, DC, and Pennsylvania.
2002 Machakos Protocol signed to end civil war.	
2003 Rebels in western region of Darfur rise up against the government.	**2003** War in Iraq begins.
2006 Conflict in Darfur continues.	**2006** Saddam Hussein is executed.
2009 The International Criminal Court (ICC) issues an arrest warrant for President al-Bashir. UN military commanders say the war in Darfur is over, but regional activists disagree.	**2009** Africa's population reaches 1 billion.
2010 President al-Bashir is reelected in the first democratic polls since 1986.	
2011 South Sudan votes for and gains full independence.	**2011** Massive earthquake hits Japan, triggering a tsunami and nuclear accident at Fukushima reactor.
2012 Trade talks between Sudan and South Sudan break down, halting oil production. Border fighting breaks out in Abyei region.	
2015 President al-Bashir is elected for a new five-year term.	**2016** Donald Trump is elected president of the United States.

GLOSSARY

faki (FAY-ki)
Folk Islamic soothsayers and religious scholars who practice traditional medicine across western Sudan.

ful (FOOL)
A dish made from cooked beans.

haboob (ha-BOOB)
A sudden sandstorm that occurs in central and northern Sudan.

imma (EM-ah)
An Arab man's turban.

jallabiya (CHAL-a-bee-ah)
A loose cotton shirt worn by Arab men.

jihad
To strive for individual spiritual perfection or to wage war against enemies of Islam.

kisra (KISS-rah)
Sudanese unleavened bread, made from sorghum.

lingua franca
A common language used by groups of people who speak different languages.

Mahdi
A Muslim religious leader or savior.

oud
Musical instrument with five strings, the forerunner of the lute, played with plectrum or fingers.

Ramadan
The ninth month of the Islamic calendar, when Muslims must refrain from eating or drinking between dawn and dusk.

sharia law
Islamic law, introduced throughout Sudan as state law by President al-Nimeiry in 1983.

sholouk (sho-LUKE)
Facial scarring that is popular among some tribal groups of Sudan.

shorba (SHOR-bah)
A soup common in northern Sudan.

souk (SOOK)
The city or village market.

tobe (TOH-bay)
A long piece of thin fabric worn by many women in northern Sudan over clothes to cover the head and the body.

FOR FURTHER INFORMATION

BOOKS

Ajak, Benjamin, Benson Deng, and Alephonsion Deng. *They Poured Fire on Us from the Sky: The True Story of Three Lost Boys from Sudan*. New York: Public Affairs, 2015.

Carney, Timothy, and Victoria Butler. Sudan: *The Land and The People*. London, UK: Thames & Hudson, 2005.

Cockett, Richard. *Sudan: Darfur and the Failure of an African State*. New Haven, CT: Yale University Press, 2010.

Dalton, David. *Living in a Refugee Camp: Carbino's Story*. Children in Crisis. New York: Gareth Stevens, 2005.

DiPiazza, Francesca Davis. *Sudan in Pictures*. Minnesota, MN: Twenty-First Century Books, 2006.

Holt, Peter Malcolm, and M. W. Daly. *A History of the Sudan: From the Coming of Islam to the Present Day*. New York: Longman, 2000.

Hughes, Christopher. Sudan. *Nations in Conflict.* Detroit, MI: Blackbirch Press, 2006.

Johnson, Douglas H. *The Root Causes of Sudan's Civil Wars*. African Issues. Suffolk, UK: James Currey, 2016.

Jok, Jok Madut. *Breaking Sudan: The Search for Peace*. London, UK: Oneworld Publications, 2017.

Rodger, George. *The Nuba*. New York: Prestel, 2017.

Smith, Wilbur. *The Triumph of the Sun: A Novel of African Adventure*. London: Pan Macmillan, 2006.

WEBSITES

Central Intelligence Agency World Factbook.
https://www.cia.gov/library/publications/resources/the-world-factbook/geos/su.html
Darfur Information Center. http://www.darfurinfo.org
International Crisis Group. https://www.crisisgroup.org/africa/horn-africa/sudan
Lonely Planet World Guide: Sudan. https://www.lonelyplanet.com/sudan
Sudan Studies Association. http://www.sudanstudies.org

FILMS

All About Darfur. Taghreed Elsanhouri Productions, 2005
The Good Lie. Alcon Entertainment, 2014.
War Child. Reel U Films, 2008.
We Come as Friends. BBC, 2016.

MUSIC

The Rough Guide to the Music of Sudan. World Music Network, 2005.

BIBLIOGRAPHY

Asher, Michael. *A Desert Dies*. New York, St. Martin's Press, 1987.

Embassy of the Republic of the Sudan. http://www.sudanembassy.org.

Lonely Planet Guide to Egypt and Sudan. Melbourne, Australia: Lonely Planet Publications, 1988.

Hopkins, Peter. *Kenana Handbook of Sudan*. New York: Routledge, 2016.

Ibbotson, Sophie. *The Bradt Travel Guide: Sudan*. Guilford, CT: Globe Pequot Press, 2013.

Khalid, Mansour. *War and Peace in Sudan*. New York: Routledge, 2016.

Sudan Tribune. http://www.sudantribune.com.

Voll, John Obert, and Sarah Potter Voll. *The Sudan: Unity and Diversity in a Multicultural State*. New York: Routledge, 2016.

INDEX

INDEX